HOW TO DO

Architectural Drawing

A TEXT BOOK AND PRACTICAL GUIDE

FOR

STUDENTS IN ARCHITECTURAL DRAFTSMANSHIP

By OSCAR S. TEALE, Architect

Instructor, Teachers' College Columbia University. Instructor, Mechanics Institute, N. Y. City. Director, Atelier Guissart, N. Y. City

(Student, Cooper Union 1864-65-66)

1914

OPENING

This Book is for the man who would master the job he has undertaken. The man who believes—"the game is worth the candle"—It is written with firm conviction that the conscientious, ambitious student will appreciate the effort made to help him to skillfulness and efficiency.

The Author.

FOREWORD

The mission of this book is to teach HOW to DRAW; Not all there is to know about drawing, but things the BEGINNER should know at the beginning. Most of the things that the beginner does not need at the start have been purposely omitted; however, the student who aspires to higher work and is in need of fuller information will find what he should have in books which are to follow this in publication. See **After word** at end of this book.

It is the authors desire and intent; to cover the subject of Architectural Drawing, comprehensively, practically and clearly.

It may require several books to accomplish this end, (The author is not unconscious of the fact that it seems a somewhat ambitious undertaking, perhaps) and these will be specific; each possessing a measure of individuality, therefore may be regarded as an entirety or taken as a unit in a series; a link in a chain as it were; The ultimate value of which depends upon its strength and suitability for the purpose intended.

TO INSTRUCTORS

This book is not intended to supplant the Teacher. It is designed, rather, as an auxiliary help; a tangible guide to assist the teacher in imparting to the student such technique and detail information as is desirable or necessary the student should have.

It is intended as a book of reference, a ready means by which the minor matters (of major importance) may be learned by the student at his leisure, and the undeveloped mind so trained in fundamental principles.

The Instructor retains his individuality, and is free to present the various problems in the regular course, in such manner as may seem to him best. However, the teacher's work will be much simplified, and advançement of the student facilitated, if not assured, by guiding him or helping to such information as immediate needs may suggest, and by pointing out to the student, at the time of presenting a new problem, such specific reading as should be done by the student in the interim between sessions.

In fact, he should not only require the student to do such reading but should also require that he should come prepared to answer questions concerning the problem in hand.

When the class is assembled for the first time, the instructor should call special attention of all students to page 77, as to the proper method of securing drawing paper to the board.

SUPPLEMENTAL PROBLEMS should be introduced in connection with the regular course of study: They will be found useful for such students as are more alert than others, those who outrun the others in point of speed, (quick perception and rapid execution). In these supplemental studies, such geometric problems as are most useful to an architectural draftsman should be incorporated and the application of a problem to practical use when explained renders such geometric problem more acceptable to the student as an intellectual pursuit. The suggestive ornament and embellishments make them a more palatable morsel and appeals to such æsthetic sentiment as may be resting dormant in the breast of the embryonic artist.

CONTENTS

HOW TO DRAW

ARCHITECTURAL OBJECTS

I.

TOOLS.

A man cannot be expected to do good work unless he has good tools,* he must understand those tools, and he must keep them in good order and condition.

It is not the intent of this book to go into detail description of all desirable instruments or implements for the purpose of the draftsman,† but there are some things that every draftsman should learn, remember and carefully regard.

Drawing Board—He must have **a** good Drawing-board, one which is true and square on **all sides,** or at least, the left hand edge and the bottom edge of every board should be perfectly straight from end to end, and the upper **arris**‡ of each of these edges should be square, it is not necessary they should be absolutely sharp but they should be true and free from irregularities or knicks.

Boards with cleats on the ends are best, they can be trued (with a smoothing plane) more readily and they

*The word "Tools" is used in a broad sense as covering all the utensils required by a student for First Year work. The term "Instruments" specifically applies to the metalic tools which are usually sold in sets.

†A more detailed description of them will be found in subsequent books of this series which are in course of preparation.

‡The upper angle or corner of the edge.

keep a better edge (more true) than end grain of the wood.

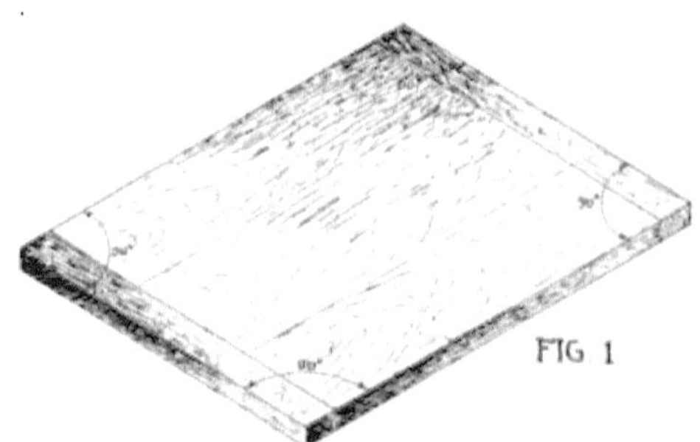

FIG 1

T-Square—The T-Square is for the purpose of making straight lines, any number of them in one and the same direction, or in other words, "parallel."

T-Squares may be used at either edge of the board if all edges are square and true. If the edges of the board are not true and square each with the other, then the T-Square should be used at one side or edge only, that at the left hand of the board. If only one edge of the board is true, it becomes necessary to use a Set-Square,* (triangle) in connection with the T-square for the purpose of making lines at right angles to the horizontal lines, that is, at an angle of 90 degrees with such horizontal lines, or **perpendicular**† to them. When the perpendicular lines are long, they may be made with the T-square from the lower or bottom edge of the board, providing that lower edge is true, and square with the left hand edge.

In general practice and for general use, the T-square and the set-square should be used conjointly for the making of perpendicular lines, which is done by plac-

*See "Set-Square," page 16.

†A "perpendicular line" is not necessarily a vertical line. There is a difference.

ing one edge of the set-square against the working edge of T-square thus:

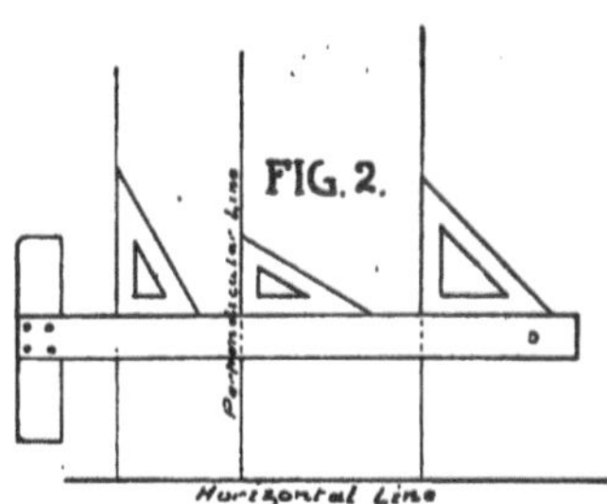

FIG. 2.

A T-square consists of two parts; a Blade and a Head; it is made in the form of a letter T, hence its name. The blade and the head should be at exact right angles, or an angle of 90 degrees each to the other.*

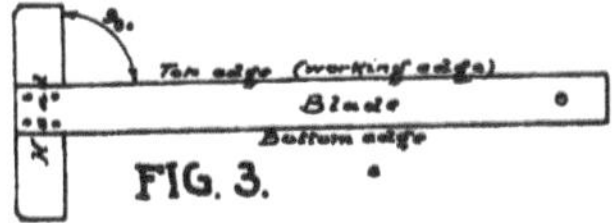

FIG. 3.

T-Squares should be handled carefully, if they are not, and are misused, they get "out of square," i. e., the head and blade get out of the 90° angle, rendering it worthless.

Do not use the T-square as a hammer for driving thumb tacks,† or for any other purpose.

Do not use a knife blade or other sharp instrument along the top edge of the T-square blade, for the purpose of "trimming drawings" or any other purpose.

A knick made in the edge of blade by a knife or any other agency, renders the T-square worthless.

*90 degrees is written thus 90°—the little circle after the figure denoting "degrees."

†Students are inclined to do this.

If the blade works loose from the head in handling; true the one with the other by use of a triangle (set-square) thus; and insert an additional screw or two to secure the head to blade.

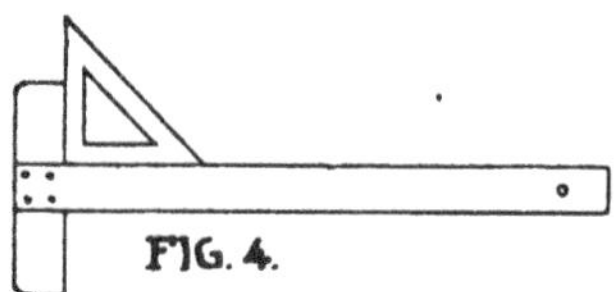

FIG. 4.

If the T-square blade becomes warped, or in any other way gets out of true, as to its working edge, it will result in curved lines instead of straight lines, or some other defect. In this condition the square is worthless, better throw it away and get a new one even if the defect is but slight.

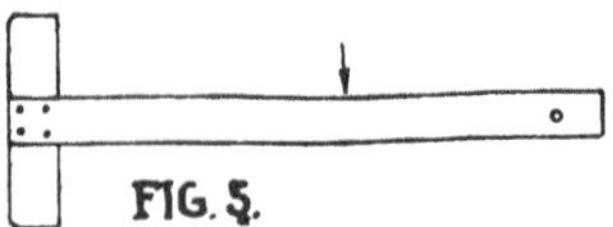

FIG. 5.

Set-Squares—There are two forms of Set-squares or triangles used as aids for drawing purposes. "**Set-square**" is the common term for these instruments. The term Triangle is a broad one and not so technical, perhaps, as set-square, at any rate there can be no misunderstanding when the latter term is used. Its name implies that the square and associated angles are always **set** and ready for use without adjustment.

One of the forms is called the 45 degree angle, or set-square.

The other one is called a 30-60-90 degree triangle or set-square.

The 45° set-square is exactly one-half (diagonally) of a perfect or true geometrical square.

The 30°-60°-90° set-square is exactly one-half (perpendicularly) of a true geometrical equilateral triangle.

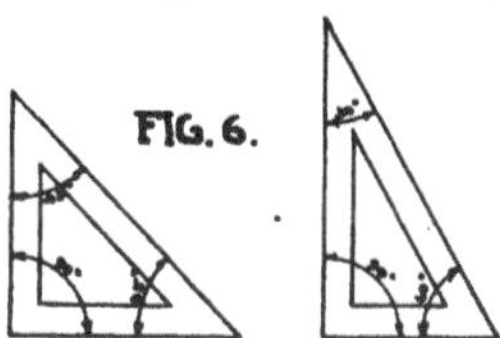

FIG. 6.

The first named, or the 45° set-square, is used as a guide for drawing lines at an angle of 45° or 90°, either or both, and such lines may be drawn with this instrument in connection with a "base line" (a horizontal line), a vertical line or a line in any other direction.

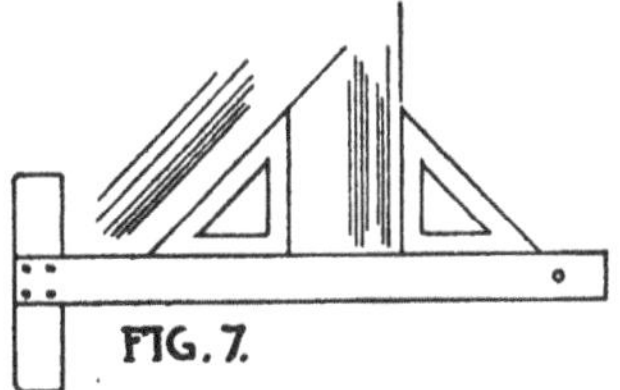

FIG. 7.

The 30°-60°-90° set-square is used as a guide in drawing lines, at either of the three angles, to any given line in same manner as is done with the 45° angle.

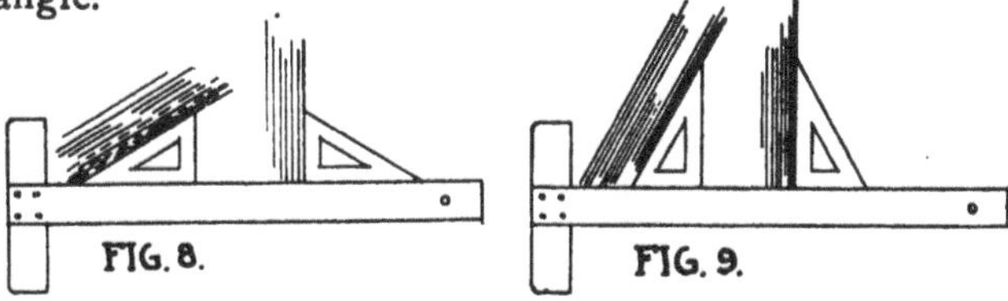

FIG. 8. FIG. 9.

These two instruments are also called **Right Angle Triangles.** (The 90° angle of each being the right angle.)

By sliding the set-square along the blade of T-square, a great many lines at an angle of 45° may be made in the length of the T-square blade, and the lines may be drawn to the right or to the left as shown.

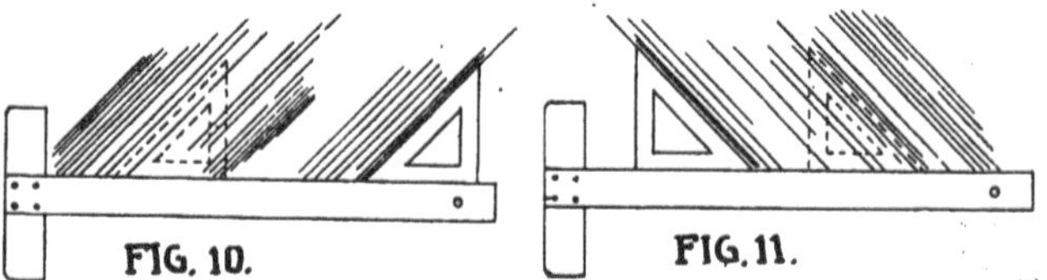

FIG. 10. FIG. 11.

Lines at an angle of 30° with a horizontal line are made as shown in Fig. 8, and at an angle of 45°, 30°, 60° and 90° with any other line other than horizontal, thus:

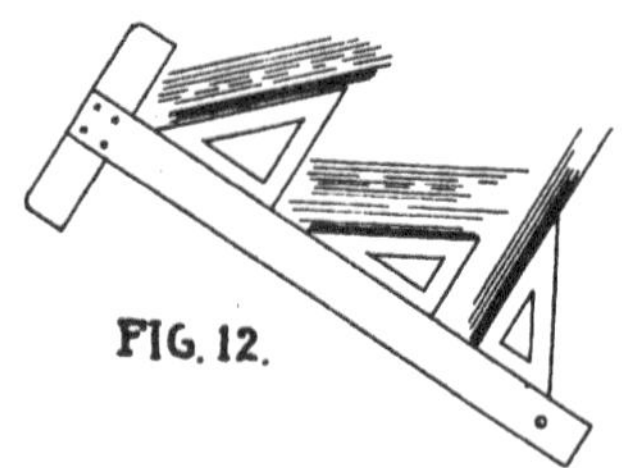

FIG. 12.

By sliding the 60° set-square along blade of T-square in same manner as the other squares are manipulated, angles at 60° can be made, and the same applies to the making of lines at 90° by two edges of either of the set-squares. (See Fig. 9.)

French Curve—A French Curve is a flat form of compound curves made in one piece of pear-wood, hard-rubber, celluloid or similar material. The first named are cheapest and best. Their use is to assist in the making of curved lines which cannot be made with the compass, and which cannot be well made by hand.

These curves are made in many sizes and many forms or shapes; however, the draftsman does not need more than two of them provided they have been wisely chosen.

FIG. 13.

Case Instruments—By "Case Instruments" is meant the regular set of metal tools provided for use of a draftsman. Every student should, from the beginning, have a set of **good** instruments, cheap tools are a bad investment, they are worthless because good work cannot be done with them, even by an expert. All joints in these tools should be moderately stiff, so they will not shift in position while handling, without effort or undo pressure. If these joints work loose, they should be keyed up by tightening the screws. There is a small screw driver or key in each case of tools made especially for this purpose.

Dividers—The two points on a pair of dividers should be of equal length, and sharpened to a slender conical point; they should be well tempered steel, but not tempered to a degree of brittleness; if they break off the instrument is ruined, therefore of no service, better throw it away and get a perfect one.

There are small sizes of dividers, called "**Spring Dividers.**"* They are very useful but not absolutely necessary for the beginner. Such tools are also called "**Bow Dividers.**"

There is another form which is known as "**Hair Spring Dividers,**" which have a spring attachment, adjustable by the working of a small set-screw with a milled head, these instruments are of great service to the Mechanical draftsman, but not at all necessary for the beginner in architectural drawing.

FIG. 14.

Divider Compass

Compasses and **Dividers** are two separate and distinct tools.

*See Figure 15a.

Compass—Every case of instruments should have at least Three Sets of Compasses, including a small spring compass for lead-pencil work and a similar one with a drawing pen for the purpose of inking in circles of very small diameter.*

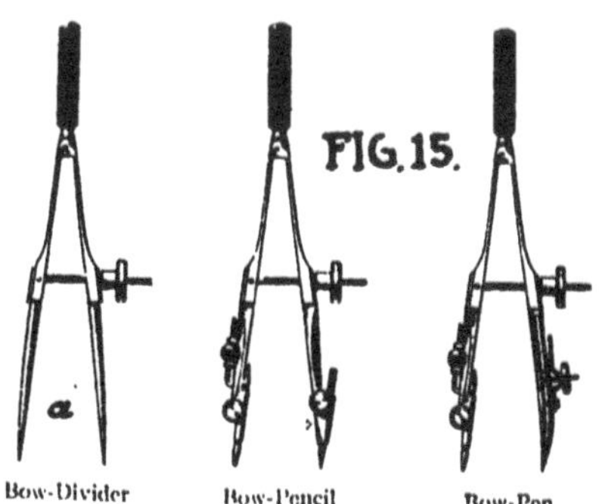

The larger compasses, of most use to the beginner, are about 4 inches long, and one about 5½ or 6 inches long. These are very convenient sizes. It is not necessary that either of these instruments should have more than one steel point, or rather a steel point to more than one leg, but they should each have a pencil leg, and a drawing pen leg, and the larger one should have an extension bar, which is used in conjunction with the other parts for the purpose of making very large circles, i. e., circles with a radius up to 14 inches, beyond that, all circles must be made with a "**Beam Compass,**" but the draftsman will have no use for a beam compass until he has advanced to the making of large (detail) drawings.

The extension is fitted into the stock of the compass, and either pencil or pen leg is inserted in the open end of the extension.

*Point Dividers usually accompany these spring compasses, but they are not necessary for the beginner.

Before beginning work, the larger compasses should be carefully examined and if the steel point* is found

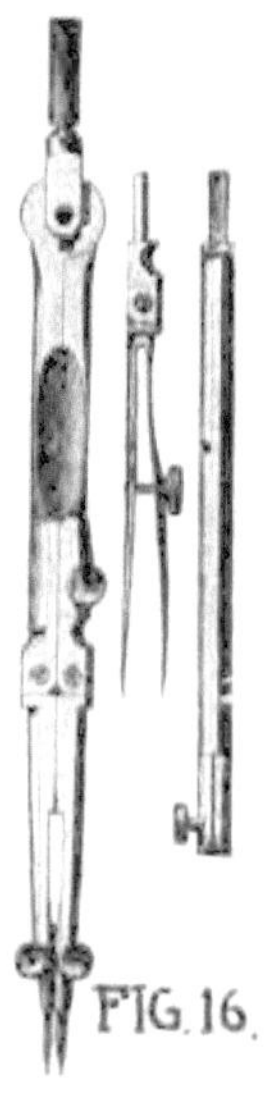

Compasses, with lengthening bar

to be a long tapering conical one, it must be removed from the socket or holder by releasing the small thumb nut, and the point reversed in the socket, in such manner that the shouldered, sharp **needle** point, will project the smallest fraction of an inch, beyond the point of the lead, or drawing pen, when either one is in the instrument.†

*The beginner rarely knows about this point, hence the necessity of reference to it here.

†It will be necessary to make a new adjustment as to the exact length of this point, as the pencil point wears away, also, each time the pencil point is substituted by the pen point or pen-leg.

The long conical point first removed, is for use in the making of large drawings, Detail Drawings, and

FIG. 17.

the draftsman will have very little use for it in general practice. This point should never be used for small-scale work. The **needle** point is the only one to use for small work. If the long conical point is used for small work it will bore a very large hole in the paper, and this is very undesirable.

Some compasses have a short spindel or handle at the top, which is a great convenience in handling but not a necessity.*

FIG. 18.

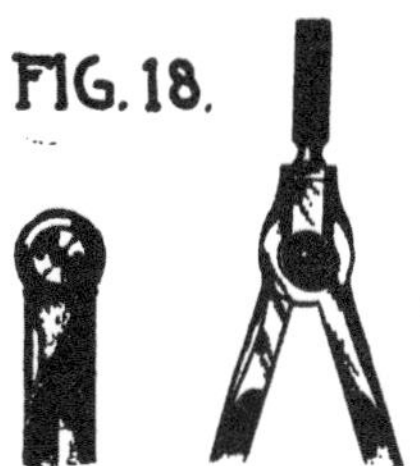

Beam Sweep—Very large circles, those of a radius of more than 14 inches (28 inches in diameter), are made with a Beam Sweep, or Beam Compass; sometimes a piece of string is used, or a stick with two holes, one at each end, one for a lead pencil, the other for an awl, a sharp needle or large pin. But, and as

*Compasses are also called "Sweeps."

said before, the beginner will have no use for these things, and this information is given here, incidentally. The value of these aids and fuller information concerning them will be found in books on advanced work.

The Ruling Pen or **Drawing Pen**—This is one of the most important tools needed by the beginner. It is the most used instrument, and the one requiring the greatest care and attention.

Drawing Pen Curve Pen

A Ruling Pen should be of good steel, well tempered so the "nibs" will constitute a stiff spring, of such degree of hardness that they will not bend at the points when pressed closely together; or, in other words, the points should spring back to a normal position as soon as the pressure is removed.

It is important that these nibs should be of equal length; if they are not of equal length at the start (often they are not), they should be "set," and it may be necessary to **grind** one or both nibs to bring them to an even length.

The Pen should be handled very carefully and exactly as described under heading of "The Handling of Instruments." If the point of pen cuts in the paper, scratches or makes an imperfect line, it should be **set** before further using.

When a pen is in proper condition it is capable of producing a very fine line (hair line), or a bold, heavy line at the will of the one handling it.

The Scale—We have now reached, perhaps, the most important of all instruments, so far as the actual needs of the student go.

The **Scale,*** which for the purpose of a practical description may be designated as a rod of wood with various markings upon its face or faces, in a certain series; each series representing feet and inches. In the form most used by students it has a triangular cross section, with a cove running its entire length and midway through the face of each of the three sides or planes.

Usually there are four systems of measurements on each face; two on each edge, one reading from the left to right, and the other from right to left. Of these two, usually, the smaller scale, reads from the left to right and the scale at the other end of the rod, which is just double in proportion to the first, reads from right to left.

Example—If the scale reading from left to right is ¼ inch to the foot, that reading in the opposite direction will be ⅛ inch to the foot. And this system is

*For fuller information referring to the Scale, see page 56.

uniformally carried out on each edge or each face of the rod of wood.

It should be carefully observed that the figures representing the lesser scale are stamped on the **face** surface, while the figures representing the larger or greater scale, at the other extremity, are stamped within the **cove.**

Some students have difficulty in learning to read a scale; consequently it becomes necessary to give a little space for a minute description of it and this will be done in the next chapter under head of "The Handling of Instruments."

Lead Pencils—At least two lead pencils are needed: a soft one, No. 2, for making notes, sketching, making calculations, etc,; a harder pencil, No. 4 or No. 5 (according to the hardness of the surface of the paper upon which the lines are drawn.)

A pencil should be sufficiently hard to produce a clean, sharp line without cutting unduly into the surface of paper. Some draftsmen use a 6, H., or harder pencil, but as a rule, such are too hard for common or general practice. The writer prefers, therefore advovates, the 5, H. or number 5 pencil for general work on small scale. Whereas a 4, H. or No. 4 pencil is admirable for scale drawings ranging from ¾" to 3" to the foot (one quarter full size). Beyond this, including detail at **full size,** a softer pencil, No. 3, or **No. 2,** will be found much more desirable.

Erasers or **Rubber**—Just like other people, draftsmen will make mistakes, and it is proper there should be a way provided for their relief. (See Erasing Shield, Fig. 50.) It must not be thought by the student that a provision for overcoming his defects is in any way intended to justify errors. But in the execution of all his work, he should aim at correctness of execution; he should also be just as careful that his work is kept as free from soil as is possible; he should remember that "Cleanliness is next to Godliness" also that "a thing of beauty is a joy forever."

Note Book—The student will find a "loose leaf note book" a valuable acquisition as an aid in recording and keeping notes, formulas, memorandum of technical terms and much data that he should remember or have for future reference.

No student should begin his studies until he has provided himself with a note book; he should keep it by his side at all times during study, make frequent entries; and the teacher should encourage him in so doing by pausing at opportune moments to give directions of information on points to be noted.*

And this completes the list of requirements for the student for the first year course in Architectural Drawing.

*See "Note-Book," page 72.

II.

THE HANDLING OF INSTRUMENTS.

The T-Square—The function of the T-square is to facilitate the making of straight lines and to make such lines parallel. It is a straight-edge, with a cross piece at one end, the object of which is to insure the lines being straight and parallel. (See T-Square, page 14.)

To use the T-square, lay it flat on drawing board so the blade, full width and length, will be in perfect contact with board. The head of square, out-side of and resting against the left hand edge of board. The thick part of the head, that part which projects below the blade, should be below the top surface of board in such manner that it forms a shoulder or flange bearing against the edge of board, thus:

This facilitates the keeping of T-square in the

FIG. 20.

correct position. For the actual practice in making lines parallel to each other, the square is slid up and down along the left edge of board, and keeping the head in perfect contact with the board at all times. To do this it is necessary to rest the left hand on top of blade just where it joins the head; hooking the little finger over the back edge of head and pressing it closely to the board. If the hand is in a correct position, the thumb will drop and rest naturally on drawing board and in contact with the lower edge of blade, close to its juncture with the head. The two middle fingers will rest on the top of blade immediately over the head, and the first finger on the board, impinging on the top edge of blade. In this position the thumb and first finger will span across the blade.

This is the correct position and the student should be very particular to see that his hand assumes this

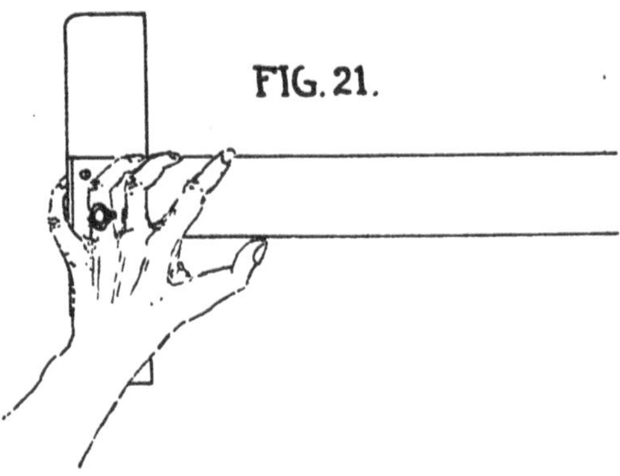

FIG. 21.

position, each and every time he desires to handle the square for the purpose of making lines of any sort.

In this position the hand has perfect control over the T-square, and the head of it is kept in perfect contact with the board as is necessary it should. When, in the course of the work, it becomes necessary to remove the hand from the square, as it frequently does, and it is desired to keep the blade in proper position on the board, it is accomplished by sliding the left hand along the top of the blade in a direction toward the right, at all times maintaining constant pressure on the top of blade to prevent its moving, and the blade is thus held firmly, until the necessary work is done. When the hand is removed from the blade in the last position, it must be returned to the head of square, with the little finger hooking over the back edge, just as first described, and thus insuring a perfect contact ready for a fresh beginning. The movement of sliding the left hand over the blade is repeated every time it is desired to use a set-square in contact with the T-square.

The Set-Square—The function of the set-squares is to facilitate the making of short lines perpendicular or at an angle to lines drawn by the assistance of a T-square, also to make short lines in any direction in conjunction with the T-square or another set-square.

Two set-squares or triangles have been described, and the **method** of **handling** obtains to both. In other words, the two set-squares are used in one and the same manner, the only difference being the angularity of the line drawn. It may be found convenient at times (very rarely, however), to use two set-squares conjointly, but as an alternative, in architectural drawing, it is much more convenient to use one set-square and the T-square in combination. The method

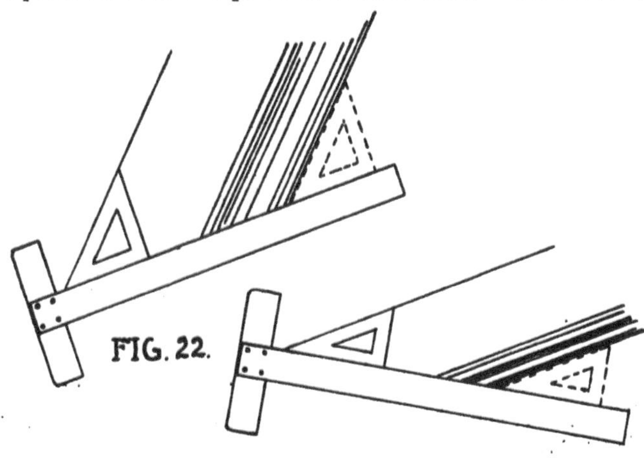

FIG. 22.

for doing this, is to place one edge of a set-square parallel to the line to be duplicated, then bringing the T-square blade, with its upper edge resting against that edge of set-square, most conveniently remote from the edge which parallels the line to be drawn; and then, by sliding the set-square along the edge of blade of T-square, any number of lines each parallel to the other may be made.

In this operation, it becomes extremely necessary that both T-square and set-square be held rigidly in place, until all needed lines are drawn.

There are times when it is convenient to use a set-square independent of the T-square for the making of a perpendicular line, but it is the exception, and as a rule, the T-square and set-square should be used as one instrument. Never try to make a perpendicular line with the set-square alone if it is at all possible to use the T-square in conjunction.

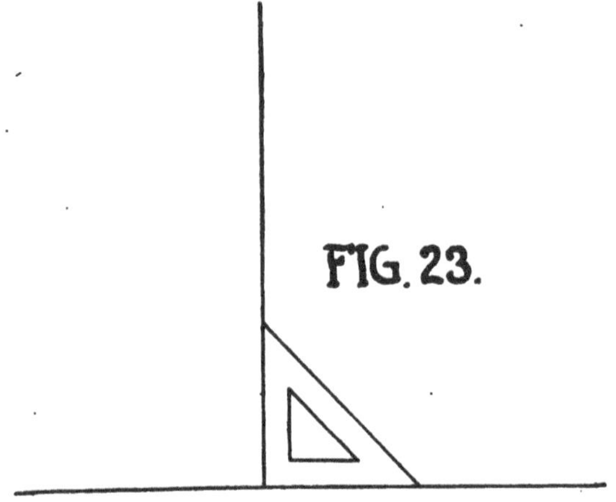

The French Curve—The French Curve is a very desirable instrument. Its use as before explained, is to aid in the making of curved lines such as cannot be well made with a compass (sweep) or free-hand. With a proper form of French Curve,* and careful handling of it, a very close approximation to an ellipse can be produced, but in this case, as is the case also with most compound curves, where it becomes necessary to use a number of segments or sections of the French Curve, the change from one segment to an-

FIG. 24.

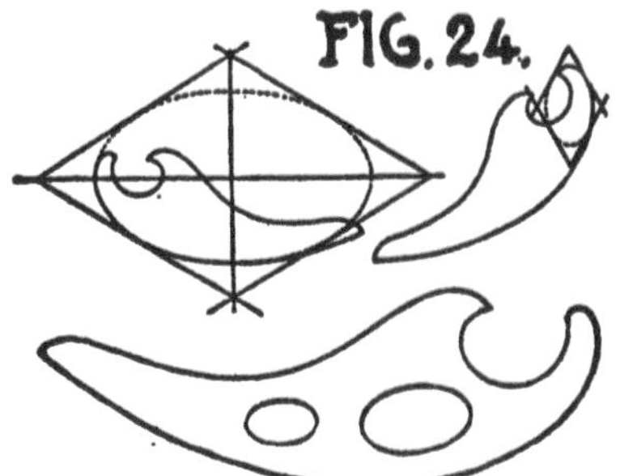

other should be so manipulated that the point of intersection, though perhaps a microscopic angle, is reduced to a minimum, if not disguised entirely.

By a dexterous use of the French Curve a clean, sharp line can be made with either lead pencil or rul-

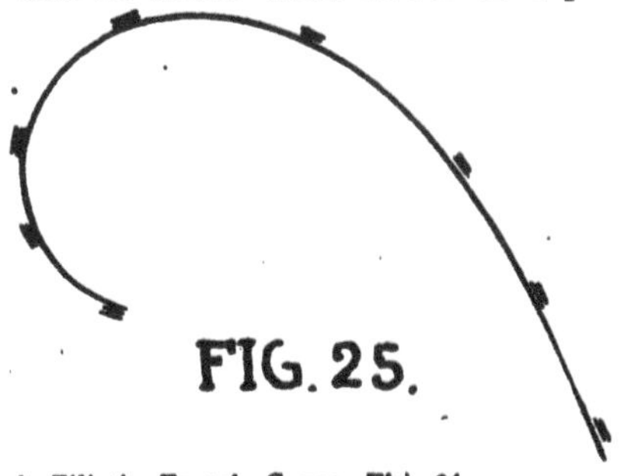

FIG. 25.

*An Isograph Elliptic French Curve, Fig. 24,

ing pen. When the pen is used it is necessary that the flat side of the lower nib shall at all times rest flat against the edge of the **French Curve.** Fig. 25.

In drawing the line, the pen must be so turned that it will retain this relative position throughout the full length of the curved line. It will be observed that such a line cannot be drawn continuously, with one stroke of the pen but must be made in comparatively short sections; it becomes very important therefore, that the union of one section with another must be

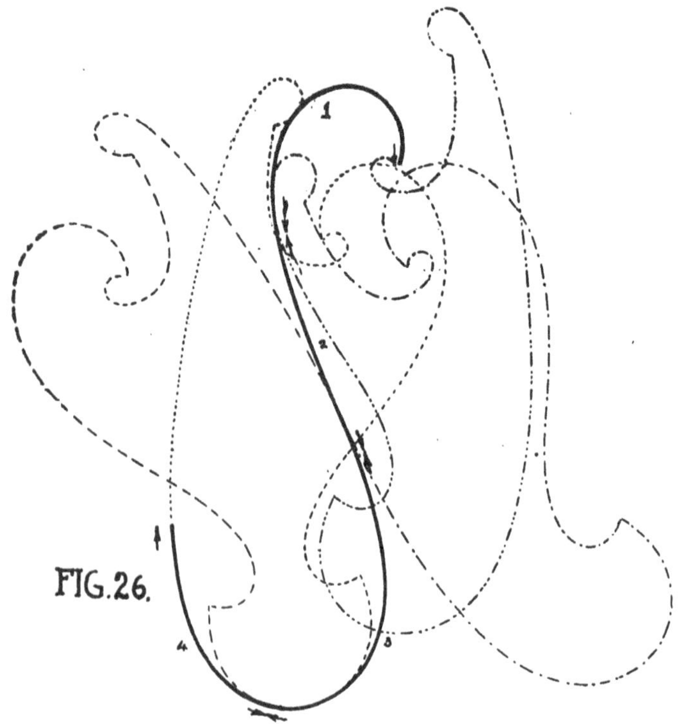

FIG. 26.

very carefully made to insure a continuously smooth line throughout the entire curved line.

French curves cannot be used for all sizes of compound curves. There are many which, because of their size, too small or too large, must be made by hand, a **spline** or other aids.

To make use of the French Curve it is necessary to first sketch the desired line free-hand with the full combination of curves required, that is, by free-hand draw the desired combination curve. Then apply the wooden instrument and discover that part of segment which most closely fits a portion of the line sketched.*

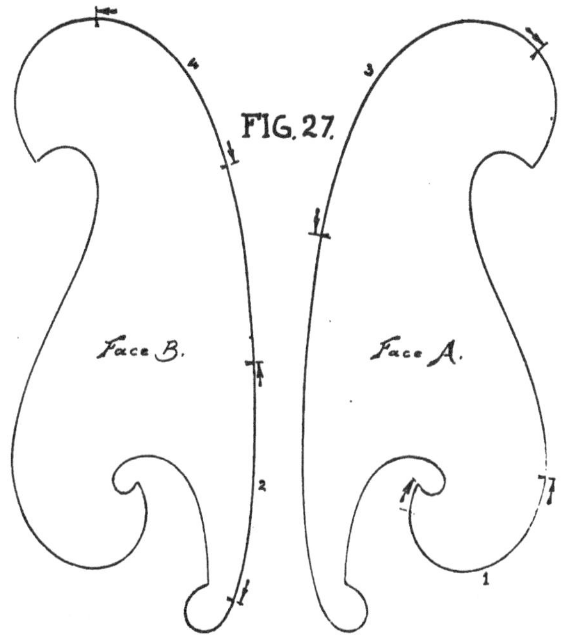

*See Fig. 26.

The section thus compared should be as large as possible. If a slight checking by pencil mark be now made on the face of the wood curve at the two extremities of the section fitted, the same section of the wooden curve may be placed upon the sketched line a second time and in the same exact position. This will be found a great convenience, especially when it becomes desirable to repeat or duplicate a combination of curves (a compound curve) in more than one position on the drawing. This expedient also facilitates the inking-in of a line covering the pencil line previously made exactly.

Fig. 27 represents the instrument used in making the example. The figures 1, 2, 3 and 4 show the exact part of the French Curve used for each arc or part of the curve. In making the joinings, care must be exercised that the instrument actually over-laps at the joinings to insure a smooth curve and to avoid angular joinings.

The Dividers—The Dividers are instruments with two finely pointed ends of steel.* The special use of this instrument is to make subdivisions of lines and spaces, particularly where it is not practicable to do so by geometric formula. It is useful in the laying out of lines and surfaces flat, making them straight and of equal length to the circumference of a given circle. This is accomplished by "stepping off"† successive spacings of short but equal length, as many times repeated as may be necessary to travel around the circle. The setting of the divider points for this spacing is taken at random, and if it so happens that they do not come out equally at the end, or where the last movement of the points in the revolving

*See "Dividers," Fig. 14.

†Stepping-off is accomplished by holding top of dividers between thumb and index finger and revolving the points from left to right, each point being alternately in contact with the paper.

motion falls short or laps over the point from which the first stepping was made;* in such event the distance from the last regular spacing and the point of beginning must be taken separately. A straight line is now drawn at any convenient place on the paper or on a separate paper, and it is laid off into the same number of equal parts of same dimension, corresponding with the periphery† of the circle, then the lesser measurement which was taken as a last movement about the circle, added. If this is carefully done, the

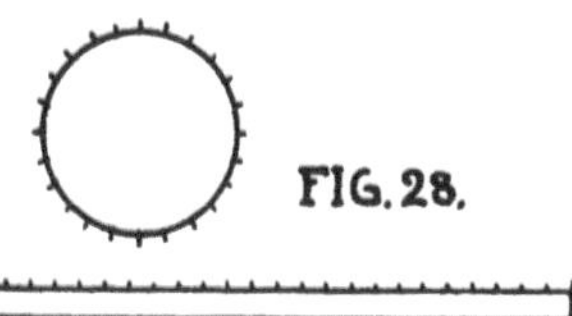
FIG. 28.

circumference of the circle and the straight line will agree. This system is useful in laying out a "stretch-out"‡ of any form of ornamentation required for the face of column, or any other curved or irregular form, also for the making of "stretch-outs" for the cutting of metal for cylindrical forms, etc.

The same system§ is available for the measurement of any crooked line.

To divide a straight line into equal parts§§ by aid of the dividers, set the points of dividers at such distance as you may think to be approximately the subdivision desired, and "walk" the dividers over the line by a revolving movement each point coming in contact with the paper alternately.

If the spacing does not come out right or even, change the setting of the points to a greater or less

*It will always be less than the uniform spacing.

†A "periphery" is the outer-most face or the circumference of a circle.

‡A "stretch-out" is a pattern of the surface opened out flat.

§There are ways for doing the same thing by geometric formula, but this simple, practical method, is best for the beginner.

§§Methods for doing this will be found on page 95.

spacing as necessary and try again. Continue this experimental spacing until the proper result is obtained.

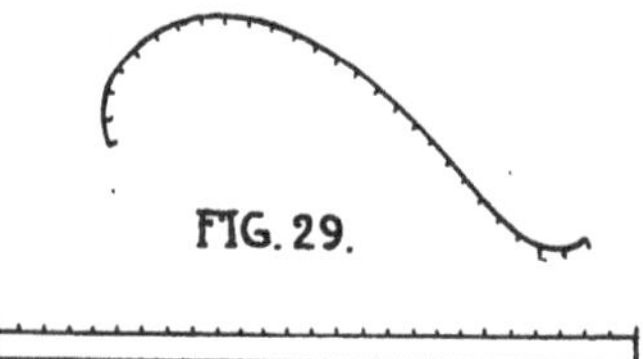

FIG. 29.

The dividers are useful for transferring a measurement from one part of a drawing to another place. It frequently occurs that measurements must be repeated, and this is a simple and accurate way for doing so, provided the dividers are carefully handled, but in all cases great care must be exercised that the sharp points are not permitted to puncture the paper.

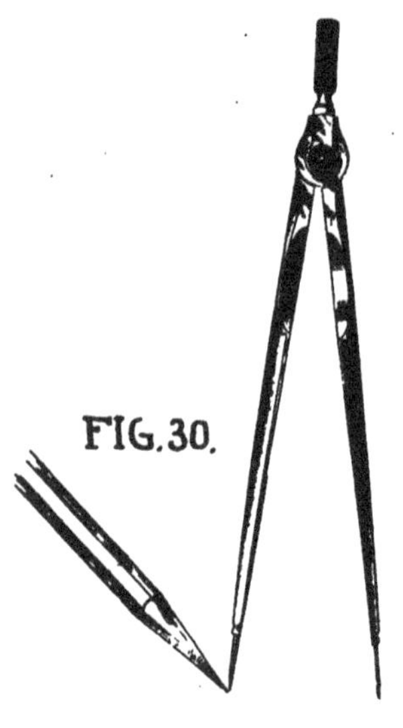

FIG. 30.

It is not at all necessary to **punch holes** in the paper (as many beginners do), such holes disfigure the drawing and serve no possible purpose. It is much better practice to merely **rest** the points on the paper by the slightest possible pressure, in such manner as to leave a point mark which is hardly perceptible to the eye; it is needed, only, until the line is drawn, and the line so drawn should obliterate it from sight entirely. It is sufficient, and consequently good practice, to hold the divider with the points barely touching the paper and then with a sharp pointed lead pencil make corresponding marks or points before removing the dividers.*

The dividers are handled best with one hand, sometimes two hands are employed, but the second one is not at all necessary.

Take divider in the hand gripping the grooved part (about one-third the length of the instrument from the top) with the thumb on one side and the second or middle finger directly opposite the thumb, squeeze the two together and the result will be a separation of the legs of dividers, immediately this opening is made, insert the second and third fingers between the legs and with pressure in both directions (one way with each finger), open dividers to the desired distance. This movement will result in the thumb, first and second fingers resting on one leg while the third finger is pressing the other leg against the root of the thumb. (The little finger is unoccupied, it takes no part in these movements.) Once this position is assumed it will be a most natural process to open and close the instrument by alternate pressure, the first finger on the outside of the outermost leg forces that leg toward the palm of hand, and the second finger pressing in the opposite direction forces the same member away from the palm, the thumb in mean-

*See Fig. 30.

time acting as a guide. (For further information see **Compass**, page 41.)

Do not take measurements from a box-wood scale or from any scale by applying the divider points to scale. It is bad practice. The sharp steel points are sure to ruin the scale, particularly if the points are used in contact with the finer markings, those indicating **inches** which are below the **0** or zero mark at the beginning of each scale.

Dividers are very useful for the purpose of analysing or working out a geometric problem, as illustrated in any book on that subject, or printed on a chart for study. The two points being slender and sharp facilitates the process very much by making close measurements. When making such examination of a diagram printed in a book, be very careful that the sharp points do not puncture or pierce the paper and thereby spoil the book, or original diagram.

It is difficult to measure accurately with dividers, because of the loss of space necessitated in the making of many revolutions of the instrument, and by the fact of the points going into the paper to a greater or less distance with each movement.

In using this instrument for spacing, great care in handling must be exercised. Keep the fingers and thumb away from the legs and handle by the head only.

Instead of revolving the instrument continuously in one direction, it is better practice to move it alternately to the right then to the left, in a "walking" movement. In this way it will keep its set distance better and results made more sure.

The small **Spring** or **Bow Dividers** are not necessary for the beginner, they do not come in **all cases** of **instruments** and there is no reason they should, for the use of the tyro. When buying spring instruments separately, the **spring dividers** may be omitted unless one has become expert and feels a need for one. Its particular use in architectural drawing is, at such times as it may be necessary to repeat small spacings many times, or to have such spacing ready and at hand for use at any exact moment when needed.

It is a fact nevertheless that this instrument is of very little actual value to the architectural draftsman.

It is also an equal fact that the larger form of point dividers could be very easily dispensed with, so far as the needs or actual requirements of the architectural draftsman go.

The **Scale** has largely superceded it and is much to be preferred in many instances where subdivisions are to be made, or measurements oft repeated. Another very practical substitute for the point dividers will be found in the "**Measuring Strip.**" (See page 61.)

The Compass—The Compass should not be confounded with the Dividers, they are similar in form but their usefulness and purposes are totally different.

It will be found most convenient to have three sizes of compasses. (See page 21.)

The function of the Compass is the drawing of circles and arcs of circles.

The handling of the compass is very much the same as described for the dividers so far as the opening and closing of the legs go. For the drawing of circles it is usually held by the top* between the thumb and fingers, and twirled (slowly) in a direction from left to right.

Use the fine needle point for small drawings (scale drawings), and the long conical point for large drawings (detail drawings).

In general practice and especially for "class work"

*Compasses with a spindle or short handle at top are best for handling.

(first year) there will be no necessity for using the conical point.

Do not puncture the paper with the point if it can possibly be avoided, such holes are disfigurements, drawings are not only ruined thereby but it very often becomes absolutely impossible to do accurate work when such a hole has been made, or it has been made too large.* Under such conditions the point of instru-

FIG. 31.

ment cannot be put in proper position a second time, for the purpose of making a second circle or for inking-in the one first drawn. Under such conditions it becomes almost impossible to successfully join the line of a circle, the finish with the start. And it is equally difficult to make two circles parallel. The reason is, that the point shifts in a large hole.

In sweeping a circle or arcs of a circle, always rotate the compass in a direction from left to right ("as the sun moves") or "clockwise" as it is sometimes called; that is, in the direction in which the hands of a clock move around the dial or face.

In the making of small circles, it is necessary that the steel point be carefully adjusted so the point may

*It would be difficult to make circles parallel from a hole (centre) so large as shown in Fig. 31.

penetrate the paper only far enough to insure contact, and keep it in place while revolving the instrument. The length should be such that the point of the pencil or pen point just reaches the paper, at the moment the instrument is placed in contact with paper and in a perpendicular position. If either pencil point or pen projects too far beyond the steel point it becomes stilted and true circles of small diameter cannot be made.

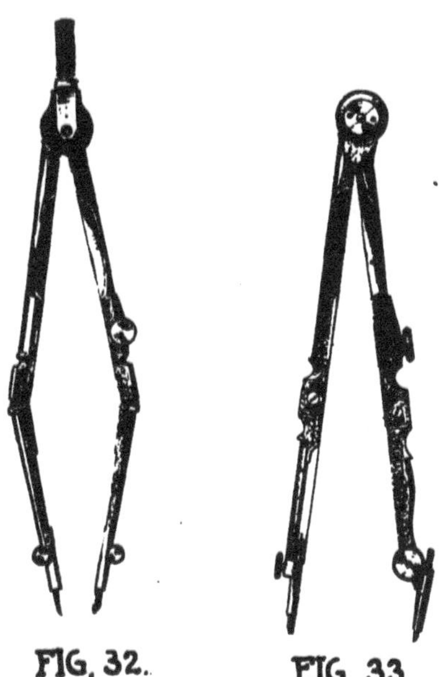

FIG. 32. FIG. 33

When small circles are to be made, the Bow Sweep should be used. The larger sweeps should never be used for making such small circles. It is bad practice to use the larger tool for small work, therefore the large sweep should not be so used, even with a hope of success by means of bending the legs* for the purpose of bringing the points close together, "bow-legged" as it were.

It calls for the skill of an expert draftsman to do this thing successfully. The beginner should not attempt it. It is permissible, however, even for the beginner, to do this bowing of the legs while in the act of making large circles or sweeps. In fact, it is important at times that it should be done, particularly, when using the pen leg. The necessity for this should be obvious or will be, upon reading the requirements in handling the Ruling Pen, and when such instructions are understood. (See Ruling Pen, page 48.)

The same conditions obtain when the pencil point is being used for similar purposes, particularly when it becomes necessary to preserve sharpness of line or exactness of points of intersection. (See Pencil Point, page 66.) But for ordinary purposes and a majority of times the legs of a compass are simply opened to the desired distance (radius) and the curve swept with the legs of compass in normal position, Fig. 33.

Draw circles, or arcs of circles first, or at least, they should be drawn first in the process of inking. It is not always practicable to do them first in penciling, but they should be so done when possible. It is always comparatively easy to join a straight line to a curved line, whereas, very difficult sometimes, if not

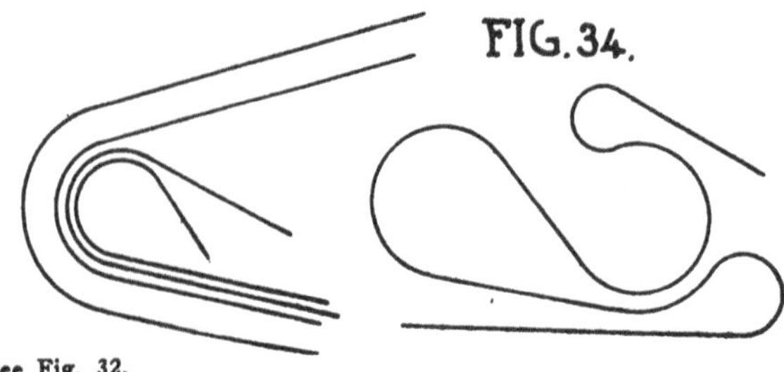

FIG. 34.

*See Fig. 32.

impossible to successfully join a curved line to a straight line.

When a number of circles or arcs of circles are to be drawn consecutively (concentric), the smaller one should be drawn first and each circle or arc added by gradually increasing the radii, by spacing the compass a little wider for each successive circle or arc.*

FIG. 35.

To prevent the piercing or puncturing of the paper in fine drawing, where it is important the centre point should not be visible after the drawing is finished, an instrument known as a "**Horn Centre**" is used. This a small circular disc of transparent horn ½ inch or less in diameter (it might be a trifle larger). They are usually provided with three very small (short and sharp) studs or points on one side of the disc only, so arranged as to insure the disc remaining in the place originally located. This is accomplished by the fact that the studs operate with a "tooth" attaching to the paper. The points are so fine as not to leave visible trace of their having been used. The top side of disc has a center point established, or two short lines crossing each other at the exact centre of disc.

In use this horn disc is placed, points down, on the paper with the intersection of cross lines directly over the spot where the center of the circle to be drawn has been located by a pencil mark (a point or cross

*It is difficult to make a small circle after several larger ones have been made, the hole having become enlarged by repeated boring.

lines), and the steel point of compass rested on the center spot on disc.*

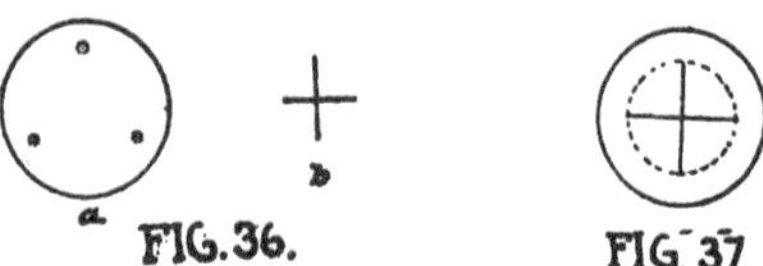

FIG. 36. FIG. 37.

The desired circle can now be drawn without leaving any mark to indicate where the circle had been swept from.

A substitute for the horn center can be made by the draftsman, by the simple use of a bit of cardboard (Bristol) or a small bit of sheet celluloid. The latter material is preferred. It can be made to grip the paper by very small bits of emery paper or emery cloth glued to the back of disc, or the emery cloth may be in form of a washer or diaphragm and so providing for a transparent panel in the middle.†

If a bit of Bristol-board is used, the exact center point must be located by adjusting the cross lines on the Bristol to similar cross lines on drawing paper.

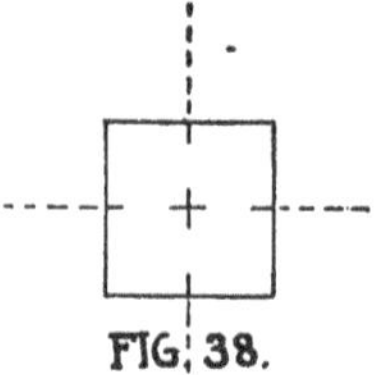
FIG. 38.

It is not necessary these movable "centres" shall be perfect discs, they may be square, or any shape, but they must be thin and flat. These devices are useful whether the circles are to be drawn large or small, provided they are not smaller than the disc itself.

*Fig. 36—a, shows the underside of disc and b, the top.
†As shown by Fig. 37.

To adjust or set a compass to a desired radius, open the compass wider than is actually necessary, rest the point gently on paper in proper position or centre point; at same time guiding the steel point leg by the thumb, then bring the free leg (which carries the pencil or pen point) to required distance by pressure with fingers moving toward thumb.

Spring instruments must be handled with the same or perhaps more delicacy.

The best way to start work with either dividers or compass is to rest the fore-finger on top of the head of instrument and with thumb and second finger on the sides of head, direct the movement first one way, then in the other in handling dividers, and in one direction ("as the sun moves") for compass.

In making circles, do not move half way around the circle in one direction and the other half in the other direction, but keep up a constant movement from start to finish, and that in one direction only. This is particularly important in the process of inking, because it is almost impossible for the novice to make a perfect circle with ink lines unbroken at the joinings, by the two reverse movements.

To make a clean, perfect circle, rest the fore-finger on top of compass as before described; thumb on one leg, near the head; second finger on the other leg in similar position. Start the circle somewhat below the top-most point; say, at about 45° to the right; swing compass as far as possible in one movement, which will result in an arc approximately, equalling a quadrant: This is accomplished by the movement of second finger which **winds** the head along the inner part of the thumb; then, disengage the second finger and complete the circle by rolling the head between first finger and thumb. It is practically one movement. In this movement, the head will have traveled in a rolling manner, close to the root of first joint of thumb. If there is a fixed point at which it is necessary the joining or finish with the start shall be perfect; then the describing of the circle should begin at that particular point. However, a little practice will show that a circle may be started at any point on the circumference and with perfect ease, by merely bending the wrist; a raising of the elbow at the same moment will facilitate the handling, and a sweep of the entire circle be made in a simple but elegant movement.

It may seem to the novice that all this minuteness of description is unnecessary; but the fact is, nevertheless, that the youth who undertakes the performance for a first time, will generally find sufficient evidence of his lack of intuitive dexterity to justify this, perhaps, painful dissertation as befitting a tyro.

Before drawing circles the compass should be examined to make sure the legs are firmly in place. If they wabble in the handling true joinings cannot be made.

So far as is possible, avoid holding compass so the steel point is oblique to the paper. The describing of a circle with the steel point in a slanting position will surely "ream" a hole of considerable size in the surface of paper.

For information covering the care of the pen leg and for charging it with ink, see directions under head of **The Ruling Pen.**

The Ruling Pen—The most used of all metal tools. Nothing gives a draftsman more trouble than his drawing pen; hence the detail information following, which applies to all pens made especially for the drawing of lines.

The Drawing Pen should be in perfect order and carefully kept. If it is not in good condition, it will assert that fact at the very start. If at the beginning the lines are imperfect or if the pen refuses to make a line, examine the points carefully, and if necessary equalize them by very cautiously rubbing them over the surface of an oil-stone or a bit of carborundum. To equalize the points of nibs: First, manipulate the set screw by means of the milled nut until the nibs are in the merest contact, but without pressure against each other. Hold the pen perpendicularly and rub it over the stone with very gentle pressure in the direction of left to right. Do this in single strokes in one direction only (not back and forth) until both nibs are of equal length, then turn the pen so one side of one nib will lay quite flat on the stone; rub gently with a rotating movement until the flatness at the extreme point (which was produced by the rubbing while in first position) is removed, this will be indicated by the disappearance of the bright spot at the tip of nib. Turn pen over and repeat the operation on the other side. Try the pen with ink on a bit of scratch paper and if it cuts into the paper even a trifle, touch the point once or twice to the face of stone to remove the "burr." If it still refuses to give good results it may need a little more rubbing on the sides of nibs.*

If the rubbing or grinding produces a chisel point the best way to give the point a proper "setting" is to hold the pen in a perpendicular position just as if intending to draw a line, turn it slightly in an inclined position to the right and the thumb will be resting on the uppermost edge of pen, the second finger will be beneath the pen and near the point, or just below the screw, in this position the first joint of the second finger will be at right angles with the first joint of

*See instruction given for sharpening a lead pencil, page 67 as to exact position for holding a pen while sharpening it.

thumb, stretch the **first** finger out horizontally and parallel with the first joint of thumb, the open side of pen resting against second finger. In this position draw the pen gently over the stone, left to right, one or two strokes only at a time, making fresh trials occasionally, to produce lines. If this is correctly done the result will be that the corner of the point (so to speak) or perhaps more correctly, the corner of the small **chisel edge** will be removed by "chamfering." This chamfering should be the same on both sides of pen also equal on each nib. The finished point should be thus:

FIG. 39.

This treatment of a drawing pen applies to all such pens, pen legs, spring sweeps, etc.

To **charge** or **load** a ruling pen with ink. First: if pen is new, wipe it out carefully and make it free from grease and dust.

Lift cork from ink-bottle and place the sharp spoon end of quill between the blades of pen, raise cork by a slight movement, tilting it forward over pen, then withdraw quill promptly.

If these directions have been followed a quantity of ink will have been lodged in the pen, but that quantity should be small.

The right quantity of ink to put into a pen at one time should not fill the pen more than ¼ of an inch from the point.

Never apply the quill between pen blades farther from the point than ⅜ of an inch. If it is placed too high and passed down with a sliding movement, too much ink will be deposited, and danger of flooding the line, or dropping prematurely from the pen by its own weight will be the consequence.

If too much ink is loaded into pen, it congeals, or dries on the pen, the acid in the ink also corrodes the pen on the inside of blades. All of these things work against the free flowing of ink. It is often difficult to get the ink to flow freely from pen; there are several reasons for this and those described above are the first causes. If ink is expected to flow it must itself be in good condition, quite liquid and free from sediment or precipitate. The bottle should be carefully (very carefully) shaken before using, to avoid muddiness.

The pen should be wiped clean and dry before using, also after using. It must be free from dust or other accumulation. Never put a pen away until it has been thoroughly cleaned, and wiped dry. With the pen in proper condition, if the ink does not flow from it freely it may be because the nibs are pressing too closely together. Or possibly the ink is not sufficiently liquid, or it may have congealed in pen. At times and under certain conditions India ink congeals very quickly; sometimes when only a short interval of time intervenes or lapses, even between the making of lines. In such instances a remedy is effected often, by merely passing a bit of stiff paper or thin card (Bristol) between the blades in a downward direction. emerging from the point of pen.

This has the effect of carrying away a portion of the ink and with it the part which has been made thick by evaporation.

Sometimes simply wiping the point of pen with the "pen-rag"* will give the needed relief. At times it becomes necessary to free the pen from ink entirely.

*A small bit of muslin usually comes with a bottle of drawing ink, but any bit of linen or soft rag will answer the purpose.

Before reloading, clean the pen, then reload with fresh ink and try again.

Students are inclined to let ink dry in a pen then resort to the use of a pocket knife for the purpose of scraping the ink out of pen, this is **very bad practice.** The edge of knife blade roughens the inside also the edges of pen blades, and such roughness retards the flow of ink. A much better way is to dip the pen in a glass of water, or put it under the tap (do not wet the screw) then wipe clean.

After charging a pen with ink wipe the outside of each blade clean and dry. This should be carefully done, if not, the rag may carry ink from the open edges of pen and deposit it on the outside face, in the very act of cleaning.

After loading a pen the point should be "set" to a proper gauge for the line desired, which is accomplished by manipulating the milled thumb nut. (With a little practice this can be done with the tips of second finger and thumb of the hand holding the pen, single handed.)

It is advisable to have, at all times, when inking or coloring a drawing, a bit of "scratch-paper," which should be of same nature and texture as that being drawn upon. This is for the purpose of making trials with pen or brush before making application to the drawing, and successive trials should be made until satisfactory results are in evidence. When there is an excess of margin to the drawing being made, such margin is used for the purpose of making these tests.

When both ink and pen are in satisfactory condition we may begin to ink in the lines, but preparatory, we must learn how to hold the drawing pen to best advantage for the purpose of making lines with a minimum of effort and a minimum of fatigue.

Hold the pen perpendicularly, second finger, first joint, resting against the open side of pen just below the milled head of set screw. The first joint should be quite parallel with blades of pen, the thumb just above the milled head of set-screw on the opposite side (edge) of pen and the top of thumb resting against pen. The first joint of thumb should now be at right angles with the second finger, exerting pressure in the direction of the second finger. The first finger is placed near the base of pen handle (close to where the pen joins the handle) and its position such that the third joint is quite parallel with the thumb while the second joint drops at an angle of about 15°, and the first joint of same finger dropping still further to an angle almost imperceptibly greater. The base of the handle thus finds lodgement in the hollow between the first and second joints of the first or index finger. This is the correct manner of supporting the pen while in action; and in the drawing of a line the little finger is rested on the paper as a guide, the third finger overlapping and a trifle in advance, just about the same position it would assume while writing with an ordinary pen.

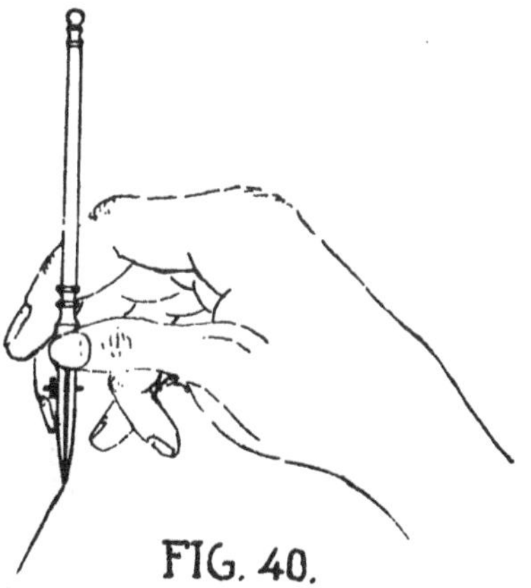

FIG. 40.

If these instructions are carefully followed the student will be rewarded by much freedom of action in the making of lines. The hand will not become cramped by long continued work; the pen will be held in a perpendicular position so the point is brought fairly in contact with paper and the blades of pen in proper position for running along the guiding edges of T-square blade or set-square. Do not press hard on the paper, but simply put pen in gentle contact (firmly but gently). If pen is held thus, the making of dotted lines is greatly facilitated, provided a trifle more pressure is brought to bear on paper by the little finger, and the three fingers holding the pen are caused to rise and fall in a somewhat dancing movement with more or less speed according to the character of line desired. The finer dots are made by the quicker motion, and the degree of speed diminished in ratio with the increasing length of dot, until the line becomes continuous at which time the horizontal movement may be accelerated. Never handle the drawing pen as if it were a "trip-hammer" when it refuses to give up the ink at trial, under such aggravation don't hammer or pound the point of pen on the paper; rather, wipe the point with a pen rag as already advised, or clean the pen thoroughly and start afresh.

Never permit the pen to change position by turning, while in the act of inking, so the open edge happens to strike against the ruling edge of T-square or other straight edge, or guiding instrument. The slightest bit of ink coming in contact with a guiding edge as a result of such carelessness will surely cause a blot on drawing.

Never press the point of pen against a guiding edge and thereby permitting it to come too close in contact with the edge.

It is much better that the point of pen should be

guided so as to stand free from contact with edge, and this can be done with very little effort by using the side of blade just above the point as a lever, and the upper edge of T-square blade as a fulcrum. This is a detail which practice and experience alone can teach.

It is well to have two Ruling or drawing pens, always reserving one and keeping it in good condition exclusively for fine lines.

The novice will experience some difficulty in the handling of a ruling pen when trying to follow the lines of a **French Curve.** The ordinary ruling pen is intended to draw straight lines, nevertheless they can be used for curved lines with careful handling, and that handling must be more **free** than when making straight lines. In making the curves it becomes necessary to turn the pen between the fingers in such manner as to keep the flat side of blade tangent to the arc or curve, constantly. (See Fig. 25.)

There is a pen specially made for doing curved work and it is called a "Curve Pen," it has a swivel movement imparted by a movable joint at the connection of metal with handle. A sort of "universal movement" which automatically adjusts the point of pen and causes it to assume any desired position while in contact with a guiding instrument. Such pens are seldom used by the ordinary architectural draftsman, they are used by experts for correct work, also by topographic artists and by engineers and "Technical Draftsmen."

There are several forms of drawing pens but the beginner in architectural drawing has no need for them. The ordinary pen is all he needs.

The Scale—This is an instrument for the purpose of measuring distances or parts of a drawing. The **normal** scale is one known as "United States

Standard," and it is commonly made in the form of a folding rule for the pocket, and two or more feet in length. The two foot one is known as a "Two-foot rule," others are designated by the number of feet contained in their length.

The U. S. Standard measurement has 12 inches to the foot and each inch is subdivided into 16 parts, these parts are so arranged as to be read as sixteenths, eighths, quarters, halves and three quarters.*

The Scale for use by the architectural draftsman is a system for reducing measurements in exact **proportion** to the normal foot and each and all such reducing scales are based on a fraction of the standard measurement, thus: That which is known as a 1/8 inch scale is one of which each 1/8 inch of standard measurement represents **one foot,** consequently, one full standard inch will cover just 8 feet of space according to the reduced size or 1/8 inch scale. The scale of 1/4 inch to the foot, means that one standard inch extends the length of 4 feet according to the reduced scale. And so it is with each and every reduced scale.

These reduced scales are numerous and graduated from 1/8 inch to the foot to 3 inches to the foot. The latter being just **one-quarter full size** (Standard measure).

If the student examines the **Instrument** which is called a **"Scale,"** the triangular form most used by students, he will find a series of markings, one section of each of which is marked into 12 equal subdivisions, each of these subdivisions represents one inch or one twelfth of a foot, according to the particular scale which is indicated by the figures at the extreme left

*The illustration, Fig. 41, is made so the figures read one way only, whereas, in the actual instrument the figures are stamped so they face toward the cove, both ways. This is to facilitate reading the figures by looking *over* the scale, instead of from the near side. However, in actual practice the figures are often in an inverted position.

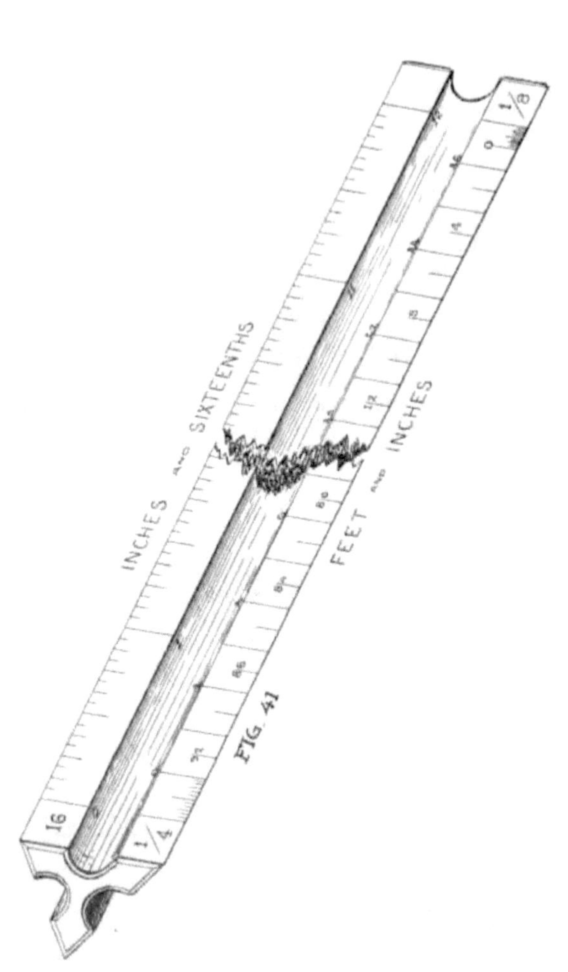

FIG. 41

of the markings. Immediately at the right of these 12 small subdivisions will be noted a "zero" mark (indicated by a cypher thus: "0"). This zero is a point from which all measurements must be read. To the right of this zero mark will be seen a succession of figures (numbers) ranging from 1 to as many as are possible in the length of the instrument.

It must be noted that some of these numbers are on the **flat face** of the wood, and some are in the **coves,** or concave surfaces, but it will be realized that each line of figures are a system in themselves; i. e., all in a cove and reading in the same direction belong to one system, and those on the flat faces and reading in one direction only, belong to another system.

To read a scale; feet and inches are spoken of at the reduced size, just as they are in the full size, or U. S. Standard.

In marking figures on a drawing so as to represent feet and inches they are followed by apostrophes, one of them signifying **feet** and two of them meaning **inches.** Thus: 6 feet and 3 inches is written 6′-3″. The feet and inches being separated by a hyphen or dash. Some use a period or decimal point between feet and inches, but the dash is better and less liable to confusion.

If we would read 6′-3″ on a scale of ¼″ to the foot.

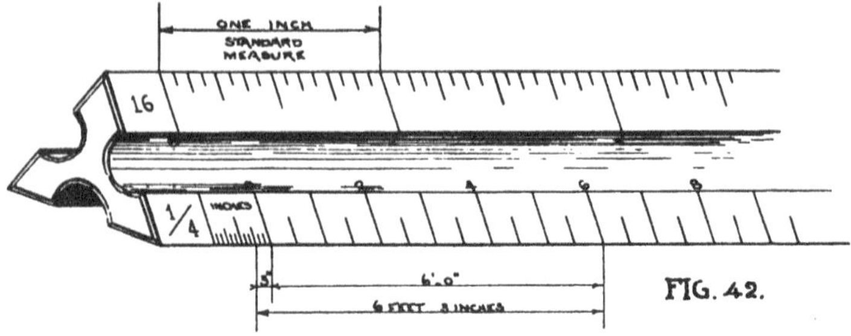

FIG. 42.

We would lay the scale on the drawing with the ¼" scale markings close to and parallel with the line to be measured, and read the feet in one direction and the inches in the other direction, in both instances starting from the zero mark.

It must be observed that where there are two scales on the same face, they must of necessity, be read from opposite directions: one from the left to right, the other from right to left.

This applies to all scales, whether the wood on which the marks are printed be flat or triangular in cross section.

This one illustration as to the method of reading a scale should suffice to make the reading of any and all perfectly clear.

There is often a strong feeling with the beginner, that to reduce a measurement from normal to a smaller scale, he must do so by mathematically calculating, or subdividing the normal measurement; that is to say: If he wants to measure a foot on ¼" scale, he places the normal inch along the line to be measured and reads ¼ of it as representing the desired foot measurement.

This is all wrong: and an unnecessarily laborious method.

The student has nothing to do with mental calculation or the solving of mathematical problems in this connection; All he has to do is to **read** the **figures** or numerals which are stamped on the surfaces of the wooden instrument (scale) for his benefit, provided the instrument has been placed properly on his drawing paper.

Never take measurements from a wood scale, or any scale, by placing the sharp points of the dividers against the scale.*

*An error very common with the beginner.

Always make the measurements on the paper direct from the scale, using a sharp pointed lead pencil for the purpose.

A sharp **conical** point is best for this purpose. If a "chisel" point is used it must be turned edge-wise to the line or mark on the scale from which the transfer is to be made; again, a chisel point (so called) will not always make a **point mark** on the exact spot needed, and it is not always convenient to work with a **corner** of that chisel edge (or point).

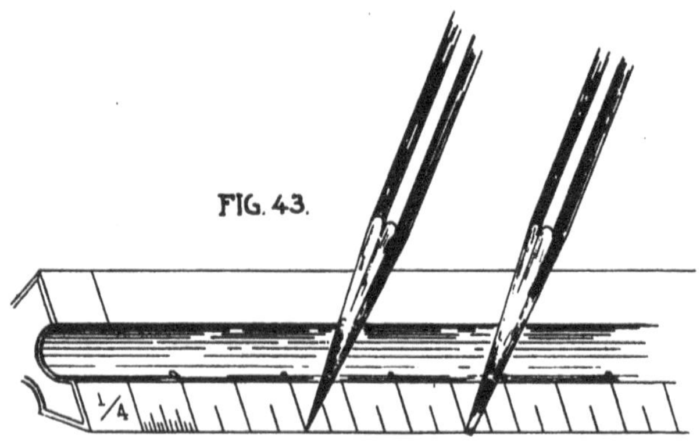

Watch-out that the edges of your scale are not dented or broken by carelessness or indifference. Don't strike the edge of table or drawing board with it; or misuse it in any way (or any of your tools). They all need care in handling and keeping.

There are many uses to which the scale may be put, and that it is put to in daily practice; several of these will be shown in illustrated form elsewhere in this book.

The box-wood (or other) scale is for the purpose of making measurements only. It should never be used as a straight edge for the purpose of ruling straight lines.

An exceedingly useful substitute for the scale, and a method more practical (if possible), and infinitely more handy when a series of measurements are to be transferred to different places on a drawing, (perhaps many times, or several times), even if a single measurement is to be duplicated, is to be found in a simple strip of moderately stiff paper with the long edge cut straight.* This is called a "measuring strip," or, sometimes a "ticking strip." To use this lay the strip of paper along in the direction of and in contact with the points to be transferred; note the exact positions by making slight marks with lead-pencil on the strip of paper; shift the strip to the desired new position, and transfer the points to the drawing from the markings on the strip of paper. If more than one series of marks are to be made in one operation, it can be done without confusion by using a separate or different kind of mark for each series.

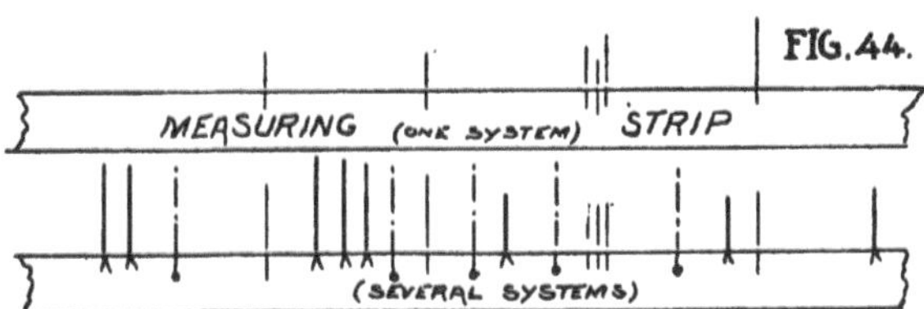

FIG. 44.

Such a strip of paper is useful also, at times, for measuring a curved line or curved surfaces. It is much quicker and more accurate than the same or similar process done by the slow handling of the point dividers, if it is carefully managed.

*Trimmings from the edge of a drawing come very handy for this purpose.

Every drawing should have the scale at which it is made marked in some convenient place, if expected the drawing is to be read by any one other than the draftsman who made it.

It is frequently put at one of the lower corners,* or immediately under the title, wherever that may be put.

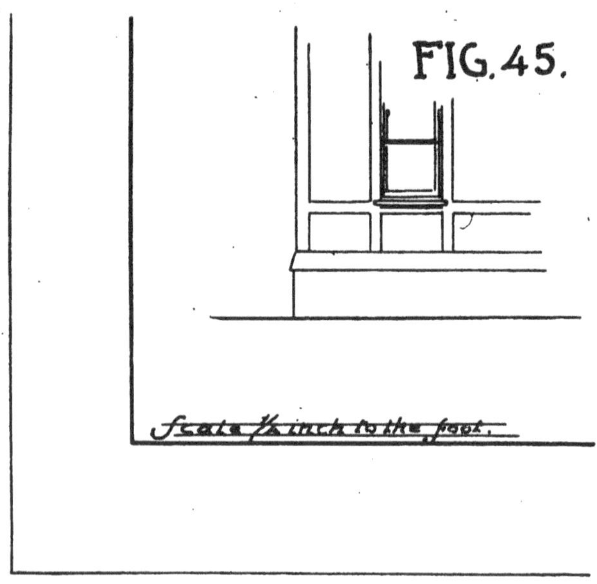

It is not customary to put a Title directly under the object always. Sometimes it is put in the sky (as it were) on a perspective drawing, or an elevation.

If a plan or other object is irregular in form the title may be placed on the unoccupied space on the paper in the field anywhere.

*See Figures 45 and 45a. The exact position is optional with draftsman.

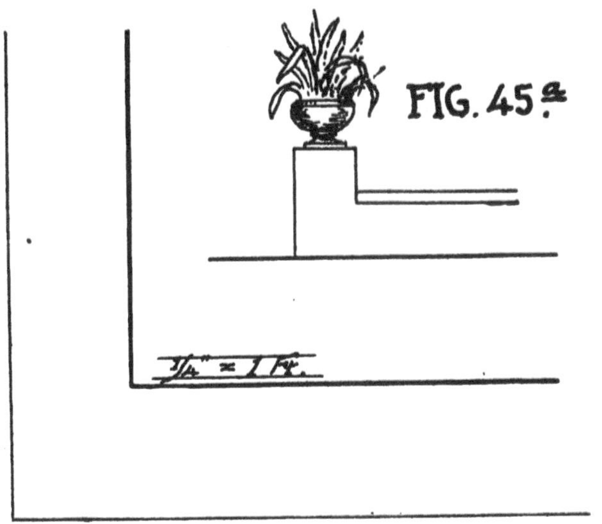

FIG. 45a.

Sometimes a measuring rod is drawn on a convenient part of the drawing, but this is not the common practice in America.

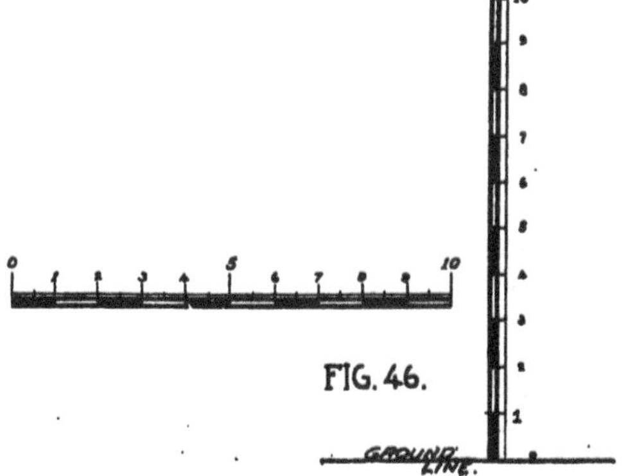

FIG. 46.

Much more can be said under this head and will be in books on advanced work—but this will suffice for the needs of the beginner; The special function and aim of **this** book.

Before closing this subject however, it might be appreciated by practical men, perhaps, if I make an attempt to elucidate, by analytic comparison between normal measurement and a reduced scale; Hence the following: Objects drawn to a scale of 4 inches to the foot will, in actuality, appear to be just one-third the normal size, full size or natural size.

3″ Scale: (3″ to the foot) is just one-quarter full size.

In this case, each twelfth part subdivision of 3 normal inches **represents one-inch,** and this **inch** is equal, exactly, to ¼ of an inch on the normal U. S. Standard rule.

1, ½″ Scale: (1, ½″ to the foot) is just one-eighth full size and each twelfth part subdivision, **represents** one inch and it is equal to ⅛″ normal measurement.

¾′ Scale: (¾″ = 1 Ft.) is one-sixteenth full size and each twelfth part subdivision, represents one inch and is exactly 1/16 part of a normal inch.

And because of these relative proportions one to another, these reduced scales are generally used for the purpose of making what are known as Scale Detail Drawings. The justification for these comparative scales or system of measurement lies in the convenience with which the mechanic or artist-artisan can measure or "**Scale**" drawings that are made on such proportions.

When absolute exactness of measurement is necessary, and where an exact **form** in profile is to be produced in general contour, (shape) the draftsman will have to enlarge such parts; that is: make auxiliary drawings of them in exact or **full** size; **the** actual size the thing is to be made.

For accuracy of results these auxiliary drawings are necessary, notwithstanding the fact that such parts may have been clearly shown on the scale drawing.

The smaller scales, those of ¼" and ⅛" are most used in ordinary practice for what are known as **general drawings.** Some architects use the ⅛" scale for making such Working Plans, but it is a mistake to do so, and it should not be done. The ⅛" scale is too small for a fair and accurate working out of a problem; therefore an injustice to the owner and an imposition on the builder or artist-artisan who may be forced to work after such drawings. This scale of ⅛" to the foot is all right for the making of **sketches, (preliminary drawings,** as they are called) which are merely suggestive things intended to show the intent of the designer, also for his own convenience in concentrating forms and to bring them immediately before his eyes while grouping and assembling the various parts, or in other words, building up his composition.

For practical work, and due justice to the owner,(the man who pays his money for the service) also for the mechanic whose duty and business it is to estimate the value of the material required and the amount of work to be done, no scale less than ¼" should be used for the purpose of making working plans; (general drawings) i. e., plans, elevations and sectional views, therefore, this fortunately, is the scale most used for the purpose. As a rule, the architect who neglects the ¼" scale and substitutes the smaller scale for **general drawings,** does so largely from a selfish or mercenary motive. "There are exceptions to all rules," and the draftsman is not immune. When the plans are for a very large building, it becomes necessary sometimes to make the general drawings on the ⅛" scale, but, in these cases, such drawings are supplemented by a liberal supply of large scale drawings, explanatory and making clear such detail and construction as could not be more than suggested at best on the smaller scale drawing.

Pencil—For architectural work both soft and hard lead pencils are needed, as before noted.

The author has found a No. 4 or No. 5 pencil* desirable for general line work, according to the hardness of paper being drawn upon; and No. 2 or No. 3 pencil for free hand work and for drawings of objects, full size. Hexagonal pencils are to be preferred because their angularity results in flat sides. They do not roll off the drawing board as would round pencils.

The hard pencils should be provided with a long, clean-cut point. The wood cut away an inch or more from the lead, and the lead should protrude about ¼ of an inch beyond the wood.

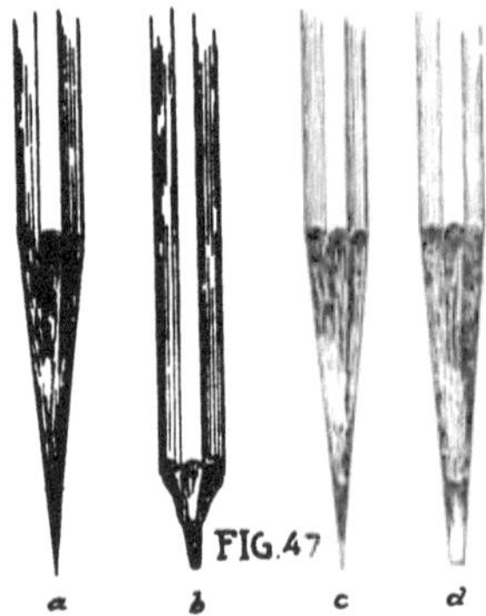

A short stubbily sharpened pencil is indicative of sloven carelessness, or indifference if persisted in, as it is with some beginners. Whereas a properly cut point suggests that refinement of purpose which should be characteristic of any artist.

*A gritty surface will wear the pencil quickly, in such case the harder pencil is the better.

From a practical point of view the blunt point is a menace and a nuisance to the draftsman, impeding progress in his work by blocking his line of vision.

It is impossible to make a sharp point on the paper with a dull pointed pencil. Accuracy of point and of measurement is of prime importance to the architectural draftsman. And these things can be accomplished only by having tools fitted for the purpose. The chisel **point** (so called) finds but little favor with the author for architectural work, he has used it for "many moons." It is true they will keep an edge longer than a sharp needle point and serve a purpose, (when straight lines predominate) by keeping an edge longer, but for all class of lines the sharp point is much better.

It is extremely BAD practice (a dangerous one) to have both ends of a pencil made sharp, see Fig. (one

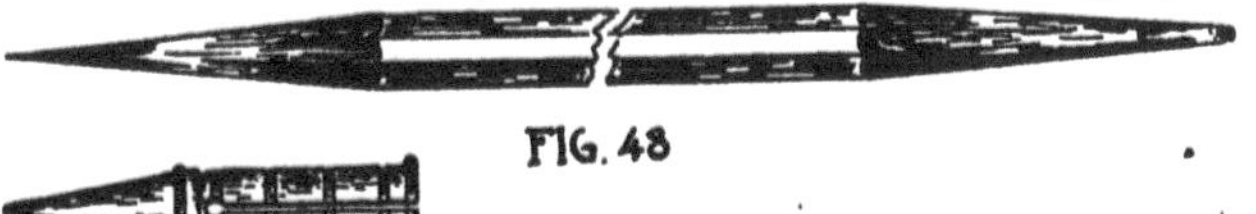

FIG. 48

with a point, the other a chisel) as is advocated by some writers. If such practice is resorted to a shield should at all times be used to cover the point uppermost. "A burned child dreads the fire." The author has been a victim to the double pointed pencil, hence this word of warning.

It is an easy matter to re-point a pencil (in conical

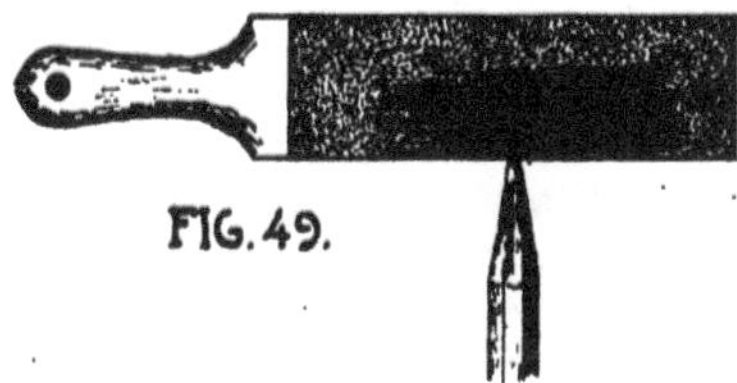

FIG. 49.

form) by recourse to a flat bit of wood with a small piece of moderately fine sand-paper glued fast. One end of the wood should be whittled to form a handle. Such a thing fastened to the left edge of a drawing board or table, by means of a short bit of string is a great convenience.

To re-point the lead, lay the pencil quite flat on the file, with the lead at right angle, or nearly so, to the edge of file: Hold the pencil by all fingers, the point end gripped by first finger and thumb and the top end of pencil laying along under the bowed fingers and resting against the root of the little finger, thus forming a bridge over the pencil: Back of hand uppermost. Rub pencil over the surface of sand-paper, back and forth, at same time give a rotary movement to the point, one way, then the other by twisting between the thumb and finger; thus giving the pointed lead a uniformly conical shape.

If the pencil is properly handled, in this process, the tips of all fingers will lay along the length of pencil, forming a bridge.

Erasers—There are several forms of erasers for the purpose of removing pencil marks, ink marks, smudge or soil of any description from the surface of drawing paper. The exact kind of eraser to be used depends on the nature of work to be done.

Very hard rubber erasers should be used only on very hard, surfaces, even then, very cautiously, and sparingly. A medium hard rubber is much to be preferred, or even a moderately hard rubber.

It is better to spend a little more time and more muscular effort with a moderately hard rubber, than to do quick work with a hard rubber at the risk of spoiling a drawing which may have consumed much time in the making. If the rubber scratches the paper by moderate pressure, or if it leaves a smudge of any sort when applied to the paper, cut a bit off to present a fresh face and if it then persists in defacing paper, throw it away.

As with the ruling pen, the rubber should be tried occasionally on a bit of waste paper or the superfluous margin of the drawing.

Sometimes the rubbing face of a rubber becomes gummed or surfaced with a film of plumbago (pencil dust), also with dust from the atmosphere which accumulates on the paper while the drawing is being made; a few strokes across a trial paper often remedies this. An advantage in a moderately hard rubber is the fact that (on paper of good quality) ink marks may be removed by persistent effort, with less damage to the surface of paper than can be done with an ink eraser.

This same grade of rubber is best for a general scrubbing of a drawing, when it has been soiled by much working over; in this operation it has the effect of removing superfluous ink from a line leaving it cleaner and sharper. (With proper handling the line will not lose its density or blackness.)

There are "paper cleaners" in form of soft rubber, ranging from medium soft to abnormally soft, and open-pored "sponge rubber." Some of them are made from rubber gum and bread-crumbs, and they are about as near perfection, perhaps, for delicate work and delicate surfaces as it is possible to be. Oft-times these paper cleaners will serve desirable purpose in restoring the sheet to cleanliness without detriment to the lines. It is also well to use them to finish (polish as it were) after having used a harder rubber to do the rough work.

For some paper and for some work two or three grades of rubber used in succession produces the best results.

In the making of a drawing or rendering it in soft pencil, as a finish, much care in handling must be exercised; and in this style of work the soft rubber is most beneficial and effective.

There is a grade of rubber, an "artist's gum" which is in a very pliable form; it is known as "Kneeded Rubber," and it may be described as being somewhat in the nature of "glaziers' putty" (white-lead and linseed oil putty) that is, it is susceptible of being pulled apart and kneeded together again, or in other words, a small piece pinched off the mass and then replaced on the mass, and when kneeded or rolled between the finger tips it at once amalgamates with the mass and can be used as in its original condition. The effect of this rubber on a drawing is, it will pick up pencil graphite by a mere **pressure** (rubbing not necessary) consequently avoiding smudging. Very delicate erasures can be thus made on very delicate parts of a drawing, and for this particular purpose a bit of the mass is pinched off, and fashioned by fingers to a conical form with a somewhat slender apex, with which point a mere speck can be removed from the drawing without defacement to the surrounding detail. The ordinary draftsman does not require this Kneeded rubber for general work.

It is given here for the benefit of those who may profit by the information. (Architectural students are frequently students of the more graphic arts.)

The Ink-eraser is a rubber with a fine grit (in the nature of pumice or emery powder, perhaps), it is called "Sand Rubber."

Ink-erasers are provided in many forms, with broad surfaces for broad work and fine edged surfaces for more delicate work.

The disc form used by Typewriters is a most convenient article. Such erasers should be rubbed **gently** over the spot to be cleansed or redeemed. Too much pressure will cause the grit to gouge the surface of paper. If this should occur accidentally, the damage done can be modified by going over the spot with a medium hard pencil-rubber.

The simple RULES for the use of rubber erasers are as follows:

Use a hard rubber for removal of hard pencil marks and on paper with a hard surface.

Use hard rubber for scrubbing a drawing. (A dry scrub.)

Use soft rubber for cleaning moderate smudge.

Use sand rubber for removal of abnormal smudge, ink marks, very hard pencil marks and the result of too much pressure.

The knife eraser is a most useful instrument for removal of accidental ink marks, false lines, etc., but it must be handled with care and judgment. The point and edge near the point should be sharp and free from burr.

Do not use the point as a point but in exceptional cases, and then with the utmost delicacy only, merely **picking** with very short strokes, and very slight pressure. In this way, a poorly drawn line, faulty intersections and many other irregularities and blemishes may be overcome without resulting in damage. If a surface is to be gone over, or a line removed in full or in part, it is best accomplished by using the edge of the blade **near** the point. It should be held in such manner as to have a contact with paper for ⅛ or ¼ of an inch in length and the act should be one of gentleness rather than viciousness.

After the knife, the rubber can be used to advantage. It is possible to perform this operation without leaving any trace of its having been performed when drawing paper is of good quality.

The Erasing Shield—The Erasing Shield is a convenience for the removal of portions of lines and detail in small sections from a drawing without disturbing other parts immediately adjoining. It is made of Swedish Spring Steel, blued and tempered. It is very durable and will not rust, therefore will not soil the drawing by contact.

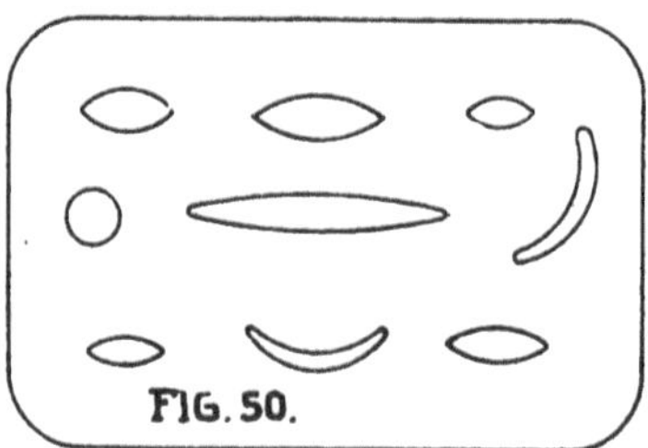
FIG. 50.

It is used by applying one of the openings, that best fitting a need, and applying the erasing rubber to the part to be removed, through the apperture in the metal. If carefully handled it is very effective and a convenience. A substitute for the regular made metal form can be made by the draftsman by cutting a desired slit in a bit of thin but stiff Bristol-board.

The Note Book—Every student should have a Note Book; he will find it of great assistance in making progress.

A loose-leaf note book is to be preferred, by far. It has an advantage over the ordinary type of note book which is in common use, in that the leaves are loose and susceptible to being rearranged when desired. It is a good plan, therefore, in the making of notes, to classify them as much as possible in the first recording, but if this is not convenient, as will be the case when taking notes from a lecture, the loose-leaf arrangement enables the student to rearrange his notes in classification and re-group, or re-assemble them in such classification as may be desired, at his convenience. Another advantage is, that sketches for future reference can be more carefully prepared and a brief memorandum enlarged upon* if the student is desirous of preserving detail regarding the problem or subject recorded.

Promptness begets confidence—Notes are an aid to promptness, also an insurance on memory.

If you would accumulate information, knowledge on any subject, **note** what you hear and **enter** it into a note book.

If you would gain fluency of speech, make notes frequently and refer to them when needed. Write what you think and think what you write. Write what you **think** you know, and you will be surprised, perhaps, to learn how much you really **do** know of a subject. If you would know a subject, take it in black and white when you can get it.

In writing, it is good practice to "ring the changes" on words of the same or similar meaning. The exact meaning depends upon the exact word used. Avoid repetition (tautology); Think: Think: Think: Think while you are in the act of walking or travel, and jot the thought down in your note book at once. Make **notes** on first impression and develop or expand at leisure.

These remarks are not out of place for the architectural student: they are all useful to him. He

*A knowledge (if only a smattering) of stenography (short-hand writing) is a great boon to any student. It is a branch of study which should constitute a prerequisite in the curriculum of all colleges—at least, it should be more strongly advocated and more generally taught, and the prestige it should carry in college, carefully instilled in the minds of *all students in preparatory institutions.*

In fact, a foundation for development of this invaluable aid, could, consistently, be laid in the common school course (as it is to some extent), while the mind of the child is pliable and the more susceptible to impression. By experience of the writer, the greater value of shorthand accomplishment is appreciated during a life's business career.

should be able to describe his work or intent intelligently; it is imperative of him he should. A clear description helps to clear understanding.

It is a fact that many practicing architects even to this day (some of note) do not, when left to their own resources, write a concise, comprehensive, intelligently compiled **specification** to accompany his plans for building purposes. Observation through many years of experience has proven such deficiency, as a result of insufficient familiarity with constructive detail and general knowledge of technique. It is exceedingly unfortunate that **architecture** is regarded by some as an **art**—Pure and simple. That the architect is an **artist** and **that only,** with nothing whatsoever to do with such commonplace things as practical technique. Therefore totally dependent on the practical builder for constructive knowledge.

This is not as it should be. **Architecture** is a **comprehensive** art which combines the Decorative and the Constructive. The ARCHITECT should be equal to the construction of the design of his creation, and the tendency of advanced education is that he will be so qualified, therefore the justification for this information as a matter of importance to all students who aspire to proficiency.

The teacher should encourage the use of the Notebook in class, he should give opportunity for the taking of notes, and even direct what to take and when. A student does not always realize the points that should be noted, on the other hand some write more than is needed (a good fault).

III.

PRACTICAL WORK.

Practical Work—The student's work should be systematically done and with care and exactness. An architectural draftsman cannot be too exact, neither can he, too soon, begin to learn the first principles of Constructive Design—Fitness—Arrangement—Position—Proportion—Grouping and Construction. These are the factors involved, and the terms are here given as applying to Architectural Drawing or the drawing of architectural subjects. Their exact and full meaning will be discovered by carefully regarding the instructions following.

The sheets of paper on which the studies for a full course of instruction are usually made, should be of uniform size and general appearance. It is not possible or convenient to make all drawings on all sheets so they may be read without changing the position of the sheet and viewing it end-wise, and for this reason a slight change in the arrangement of marginal lines must be made to accommodate both necessary forms. It is desirable that as many as possible should be read from one direction.*

It is a good plan to so arrange the marginal lines that the sheets may be fastened into book form by metal fasteners or otherwise, and for this purpose it is necessary to have the binding margin greater than elsewhere. The greater margin should be at the left

*A drawing should not be made or lettered so it becomes necessary to view it from the left hand end. It should at all times be read from the front or right hand end.

end of the sheet when it is viewed from the long side, and at the top of the sheet when looked at from the end.

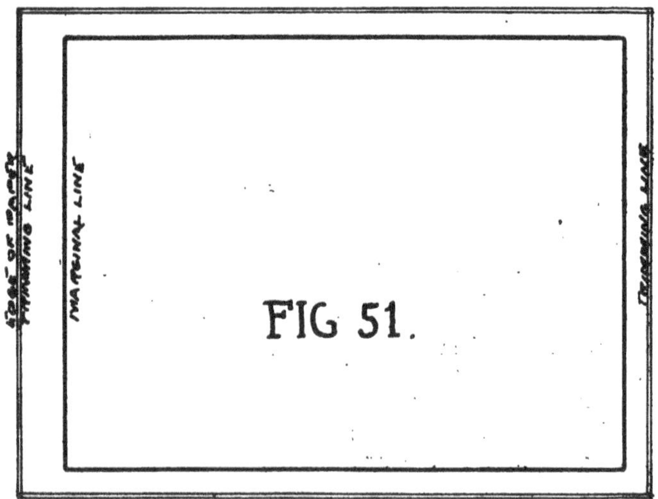

FIG 51.

The paper on which these charts are to be made should be 11 inches wide by 15 inches long, it may vary a trifle, and it may not be true as to squareness, therefore, the drawings should be so made that they can be **trimmed**,* thereby made uniform as to size and shape.

Having obtained our paper the first thing to be learned is to properly put it on the drawing board that it may be in fit condition for working on, a very simple thing apparently, but there is a right way for doing it and that way should be learned at the first handling of the paper.

*The trimming lines and all marginal lines are shown on all charts throughout this book.

Place the sheet on board about 3 or 4 inches from the left edge of board (the working edge), and about

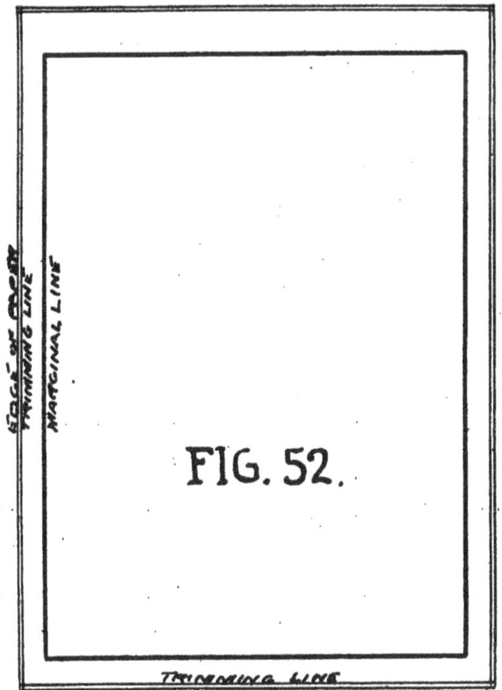

FIG. 52.

5 or 6 inches from the bottom edge of board. The latter to insure a resting place for the hand when working at or near the lower edge of paper.

Secure the upper left hand corner of paper to board with a thumb tack, about 1/16 of an inch from edge of paper.* Place the T-square on the paper, with its

*Tack holes should not appear after drawing is finished and trimmed.

head bearing snugly against the left edge of board in close contact the full length of head.

Square the top edge of paper with the T-square. The best way to do this is to move the T-square with the left hand resting on head of square (see illustration page 30), grip the lower right hand corner of paper between thumb and first finger, right hand, and move the sheet up and down; by this movement it will be found a very simple matter to square the paper by making the top edge parallel with the top edge of T-square blade. The thumb-tack acts as a pivot, hence the paper moves easily to its place.

Hold paper in this position with right hand, and slide T-square down an inch or so, and then secure the right hand upper corner of paper with a second thumb-tack. The T-square may now be removed, and each lower corner secured in turn by the insertion of a thumb-tack, to do this rest the palm of the hand on paper about midway and brush gently in the direction of the corner to be secured, repeat the movement for the fourth and last corner.

If this has been properly done the paper will have been put down as flat as is possible, without "stretching."*

If a drawing is left on a board a day, or longer (even over-night sometimes), moisture from the atmosphere may so affect the paper that readjustment may become necessary before resuming the work of drawing to insure the lines being parallel. When it does become necessary that readjustment should be made it is best done by lifting three tacks and repeating the process described for first laying the paper.

We are now ready to make **lines** and we will make the first one by using the T-square as a straight edge.

*The stretching of paper is a process not needed by the beginner, therefore not explained in this book.

Press the head of square firmly against the left edge of board (see page 30) slide it up until top edge of blade is ⅛ of an inch from top edge of paper and draw a line, left to right, using a No. 4 or No. 5 lead pencil which must be sharply pointed (see page 66).

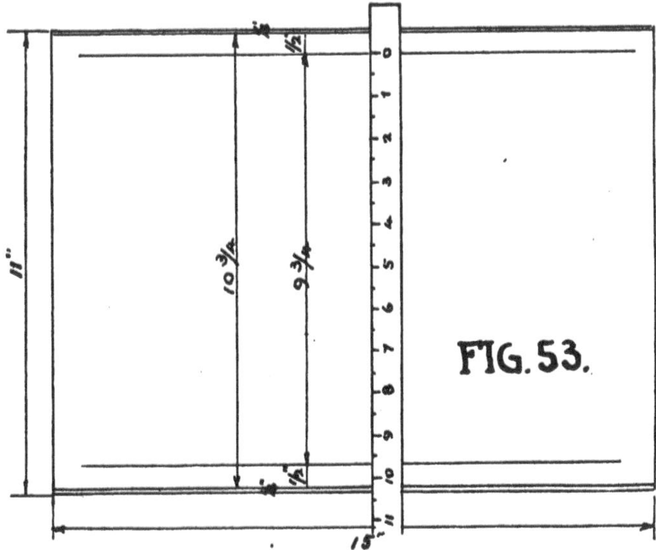

FIG. 53.

Do not press hard on the paper but make a line sufficiently firm and strong that it may be easily seen in the light under which you are working.

Never put the point of the pencil to the tongue or mouth for the purpose of moistening the lead; it is absolutely unnecessary, and an exceedingly bad habit. Use the pencil in its natural condition, dry. The only thing you need have anxiety about is the **point.** Keep a sharp eye to the pencil point that it may itself be **sharp.** Having drawn the first line, place the scale (see page 80) on paper at right angles to the line, and measure off ½ inch, "standard measurement" (actual size), and draw a second line. For the purpose

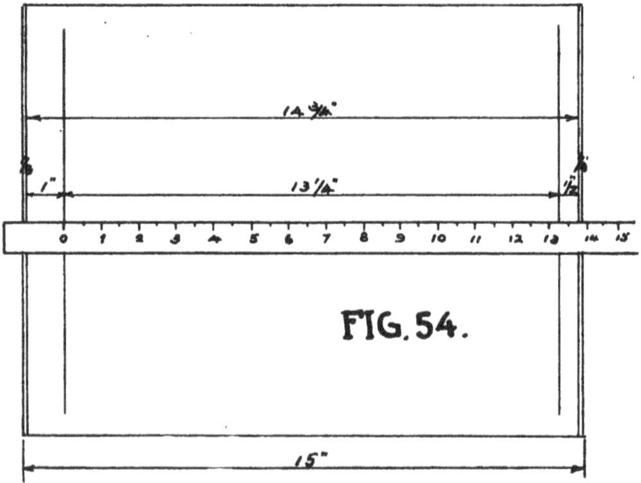

FIG. 54.

of making this measurement use that edge of the scale which has one system of markings only; i. e., One foot divided into 12 inches and each inch subdivided into 16 equal parts. This is the standard scale of measurement, therefore, at all times when the **standard scale** or **standard measurement** is referred to it means this particular marking on the box-wood instrument. From the second line, measure in a direction downward, a space of 9¾ inches and draw a third line.

Space off ½ inch below this third line and draw the fourth which will be the bottom line and should be a fraction from the bottom edge of paper.

Now, start at the left edge of paper and draw a vertical line, i. e., a line which is perpendicular to the four lines already drawn. Place it about ⅛ of an inch from edge of paper.

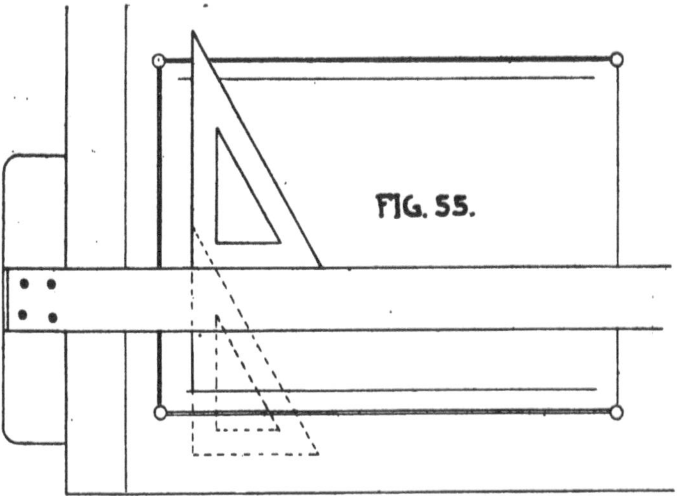

FIG. 55.

If the drawing board is square and true (see page 13), the T-square may be used at the bottom edge of board for the purpose of making the border lines which are perpendicular. If the board is not square and true, these perpendicular lines must be made by using the T-square in its normal position at the left edge of board together with a set-square, (see page 82). Use that set-square which has the longest side or edge, and if that side or edge is not long enough to reach the full length of the required line, it will become necessary to slide the T-square a trifle and move the set-square with it, at same time keeping both in perfect contact.

From this first perpendicular line draw another parallel to it and 1 inch from it. Then measure 13¼ inches in a horizontal direction and draw a third perpendicular line; measure ½ inch more and draw the fourth and last perpendicular line, which will or should be about ⅛ of an inch from the right hand edge of paper. Now with the pencil rubber remove the over-shot lines at all corners leaving the joinings at the corners true, square and clean, (see page 225).

The finished result will be as shown in Fig. 56.

Title—It is desirable there should be a marking of some kind on each drawing, as identification, or explanatory of the subject of the drawing, and this

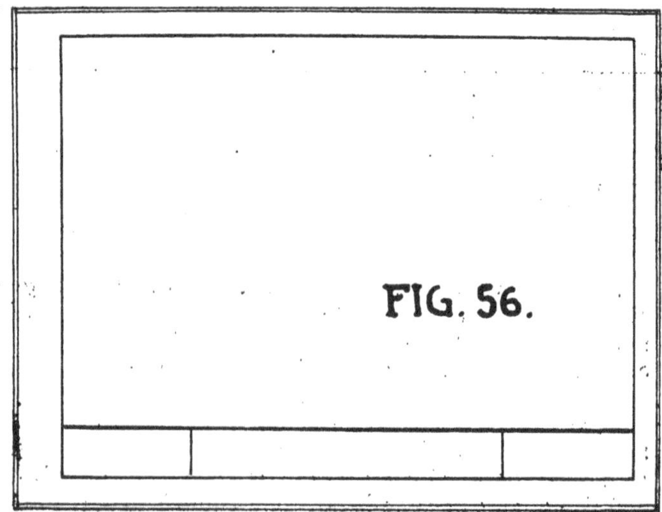

marking is called the **Title.** To provide a place for this title we will lay off another line 1 inch above the bottom margin line and parallel to it, i. e., horizontal.

At either end of the space so laid off, mark off a smaller panel 2½ inches long, thus forming three separate panels.

One at the left, 1 inch high by 2½ inches long. A middle panel 1 inch high by 8¼ inches long and a third (at the extreme right) 1 inch high by 2½ inches long. This is the form in whch all sheets for the full class series should be laid out, except, where it becomes necessary to turn the sheet endwise, in which case the title panel should be at that end of the paper which will be the bottom when in position for proper reading.

Never put reading matter or figures on a drawing as shown in Fig. 59, it is exceedingly bad practice. A drawing should not be so labeled that it becomes

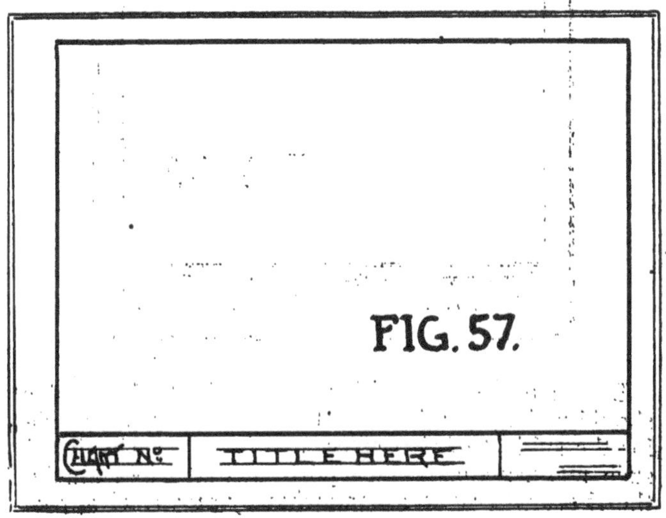

FIG. 57.

necessary to turn it to the left for the purpose of reading; it should always be turned from the left to the right; it is the most natural and the most convenient way of handling a print.

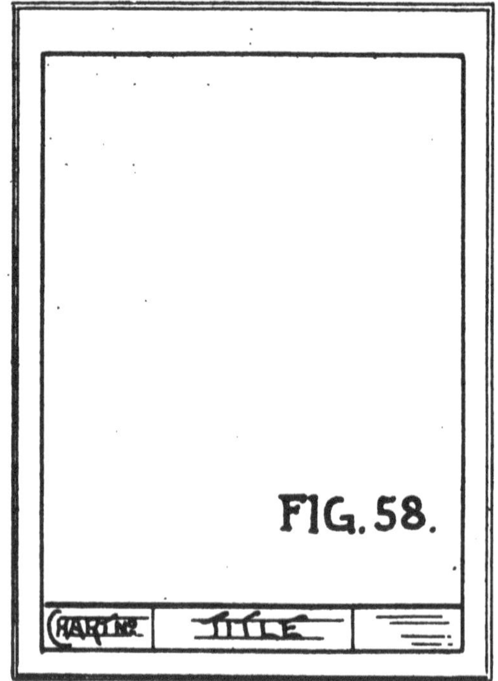

FIG. 58.

Before proceeding with any one chart, the student should make a rough calculation as to the space needed for the subject of that chart, and lay out each view in such manner and in such position that when finished the sheet will have a somewhat symmetrical appear-

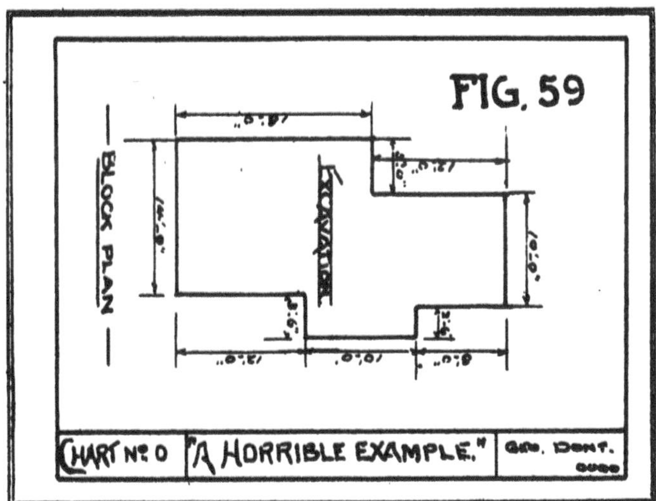

ance. There should be a certain **balance** to the various parts or views shown on each and every sheet.

For example: We will take the First Chart of the series as presented to the students of the beginners course at Mechanics Institute, N. Y. City. Fig. 60 shows what the completed drawing is to be; and Fig. 61 shows the method of "blocking-out," so the several diagrams will be distributed with balance and symmetry.*

This "blocking out" of work, should be done by first discovering as nearly as possible the space needed:

Instructor can give this information on black-board, or otherwise as he prefers. In this case the inner-most panel will be 7½ inches high and 11 inches long.

Having done this, find the exact centre of the space to be occupied by the entire drawing, this is done by placing the upper edge of T-square blade in contact

*See next page.

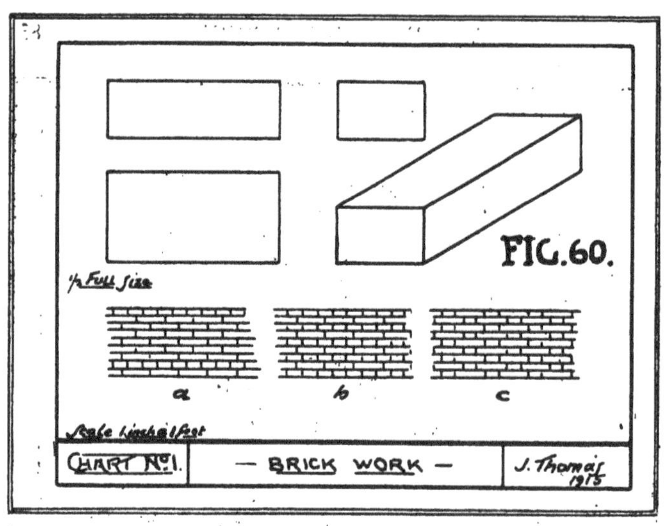

FIG. 60.

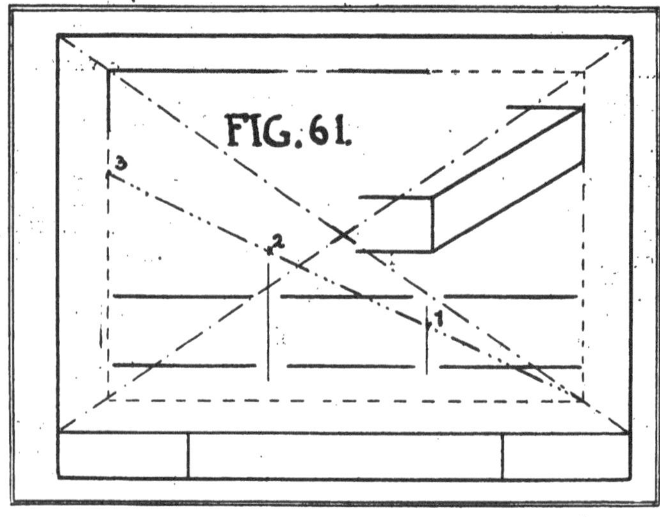

FIG. 61.

with diagonal corners, say the lower left and upper right (marked a, b, Fig. 62), and draw a short straight line as near the centre of panel as can be approximated by eye measurement. Shift the edge of T-square blade to points c, d, and draw a second short line crossing the first.

The intersection of these two short lines will indicate the exact centre of the panel. Remove the T-square and place it flat on board and draw a horizontal line through the point of intersection, marked e, Fig. 63. Reverse T-square as shown by dotted lines on dia-

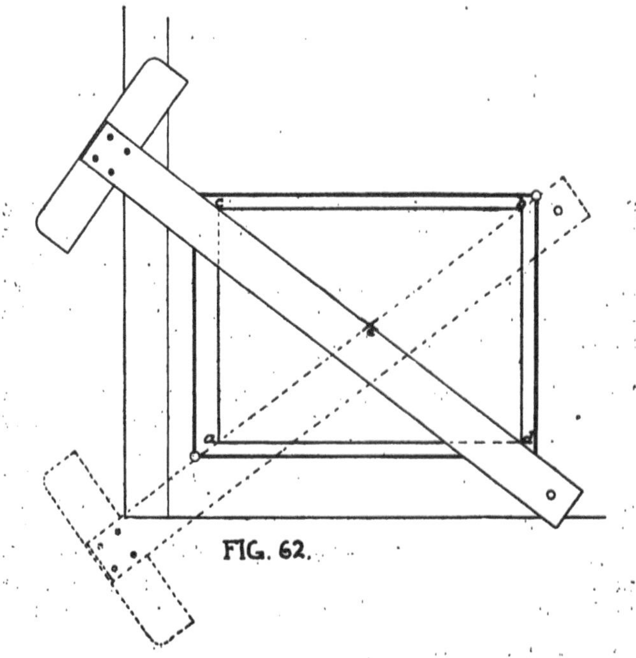

FIG. 62.

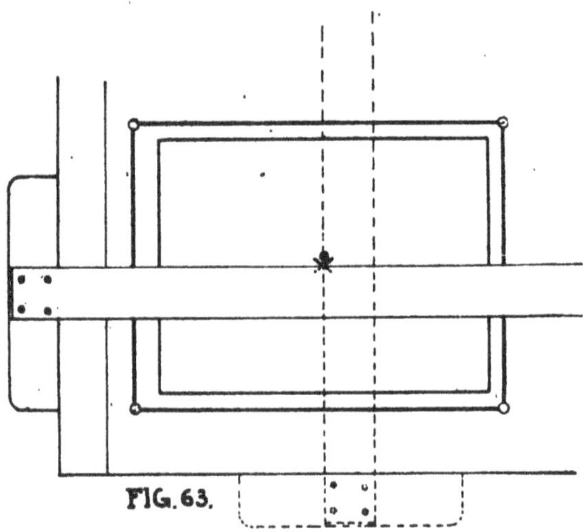

FIG. 63.

gram, and draw a perpendicular line also passing through e, and the two lines so drawn will constitute the horizontal and perpendicular **centre lines,** technically called the horizontal axis and the perpendicular axis; or, the long line is called the **major axis,** and the shorter one the **minor axis** of the panel.

It will be noted that this panel is not square, but longer in one direction than it is in the other, and since it is formed of straight lines ("right lines," as they are called), this plane is called a **parallelogram.** A parallelogram is a geometric figure of four sides, or a figure constructed with four lines in two directions, two of which are always parallel.*

We have previously drawn the border lines, and it is now our purpose to locate the object or subject we desire to represent by the various diagrams. We shall

*Figure 64, shows types of parallelograms.

place them (group them), so they shall have a relative value; that is, our drawing should make clearly understood the relation that one diagram bears to another, and for this purpose the diagrams should themselves

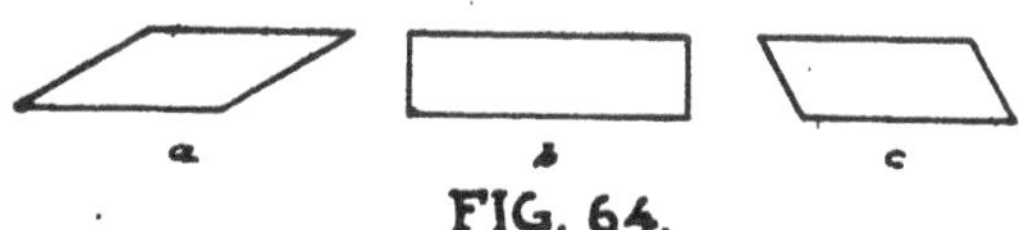

FIG. 64.

be so placed and arranged as to be self-explanatory. To illustrate: (Fig. 60). The principal object on our first study chart is a common brick, and it is represented by four separate diagrams (parallelograms). The brick is an ordinary one and is called a "common brick" (it is one used for ordinary and rough work), its dimensions therefore are, length 8", width 4", height 2".† It is, what is known geometrically, as a "solid" (a thing with height, depth and breadth), a form which occupies three dimensions in space. The limit of possibility in dimensioning of objects. It is a **prism** type of solids and because its several faces are parallelograms in form (longer one way than another, with straight lines and **square corners**), it is that type called "rectangular." (see Fig. 64). It is, therefore, a **rectangular prism.** The two larger faces or planes of this prism or brick are described as being **"beds,"** on one of which it usually rests when placed in a wall to receive another brick above it. The bed dimensions of a common brick are 4" x 8".

There are four other faces or planes to a brick, two of them are short and two are longer, the shorter ones are called "heads" or "headers" (when they are built in the wall with the short end to the front or in full

†Bricks vary in size, but these measurements are standard for common brick.

view. The two longer faces are called "stretchers" when placed in similar position in a wall. The heads measure 2"x4" while the "stretchers" are 2"x8".

To show this brick and fully describe it by geometric diagrams requires three views, one of the bed, one of the stretcher and one of the head, and to make the diagrams susceptible to intelligent "reading" (under-

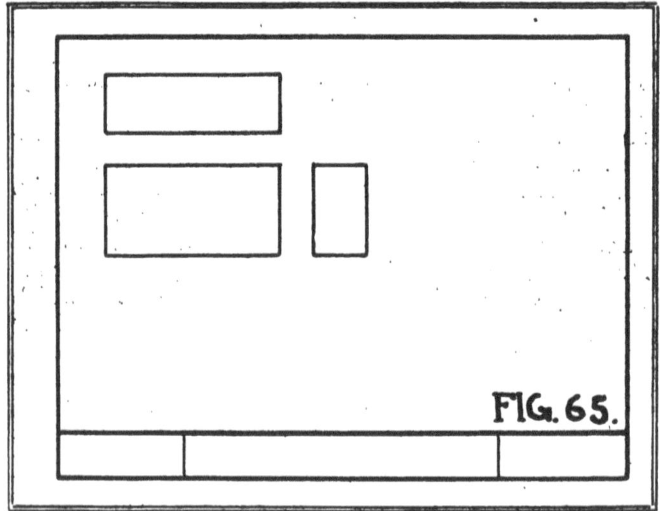

FIG. 65.

standing) they must be so placed on the paper as to show their geometric relation one to the other, and to that end by reference to (Chart No. 1, Fig. 60), it will be noticed that the bed is first shown as a PLAN, because it indicates the measurement on the ground, as it were, and immediately above it, parallel with its longer dimension is placed a view of the longer face (stretcher) which view is called an ELEVATION, because of the fact that it represents or indicates height as well as breadth. It is a FRONT ELEVATION because it represents the principal face of the brick. Its position explains its relation to the bed. The third diagram represents the end or head of brick, therefore it is placed at the end of the front elevation, with its greater dimension parallel with the greater length of the front elevation.

Sometimes it is convenient and even desirable the arrangement of these three views should be different from that shown; as example: see Fig. 65. In this case the Plan and Front Elevation are placed in same relative position as already shown, while the end view or End Elevation is shown in a different position; i. e., at the end of the Plan with its longer dimension parallel with the line of same measurement on the plan. The two Elevations now occupy positions relative to

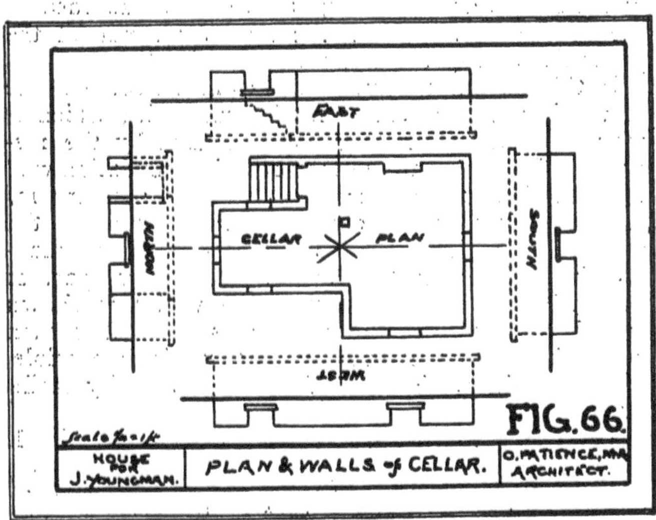

FIG. 66.

the Plan in what is termed in descriptive geometry as "revolved positions." The planes of the elevations are **revolved** (laid flat) from the plane of the bed or plan, in the direction of their horizontal axis, each in its own specific plane and relative space. This latter arrangement is commonly resorted to as being a most convenient method for the making of "block-plans and elevations" for the special purpose or use by men of a limited trade or for a limited part of a building.

It is a form or arrangement very popular if not in quite general vogue with the Mechanical or Technical draftsman and one extremely useful to him.

In general practice in architectural drawing, however, each view is made independent of all others, so far as plans and elevations are concerned, in the majority of instances each view or drawing being on a separate sheet of paper and its relation to the others indicated by its title. Fig 66 will give an idea of the usefulness to the architectural draftsman of the particular arrangement under discussion.*

In this case its specific value lies in the convenience in making the drawing and the ease with which it may be read (understood) and handled by the mechanic. The illustration represents the foundation wall for a small house, and in it, all that is necessary for temporary use of the excavator and mason for the purpose of building the foundation walls and making them ready for the superstructure (that part of the building above the foundation walls) is shown on this diagram, and the parts are so related to each other that misunderstanding of them is impossible, its use to the workman is therefore materially facilitated.

There is a fourth diagram shown on Chart No. 1.

*Fig. 66, is an exceptional instance where it is not only permissible but correct to invert a title as shown by the word "West." If that word occupied any other position it would not be in its proper place relative to the view referred to.

It is what is called an Isometric* View of the brick. Such views are not as a rule shown by architectural plans, though very useful and should form a feature in common practice. Its purpose here is to show all three views, the geometric diagrams assembled in one view, each in its relative place to represent the solid brick.

A peculiarity of this type of illustration is, that it not only shows the complete and perfect form of the brick, but in such way that all of its various faces may be correctly measured by the mere application of a scale or rule, that is to say: It can be scaled in three dimensions of a solid and accurate measurements so taken in each direction. In this respect (the ability to take accurate measurements) an Isometric view differs from a Perspective view (a more perfect form of **picture). In the last named representation** measurements cannot be taken except by one thoroughly skilled in the particular art of Linear Perspective, and by him, only, through a system of expert constructive handling such as is far beyond the comprehension of the beginner in architectural drawing. Briefly comparing the two: Isometry is a geometrical picture. Perspective is an Optical picture. The comparison is given here because the tyro is very prone to confuse them for want of understanding.

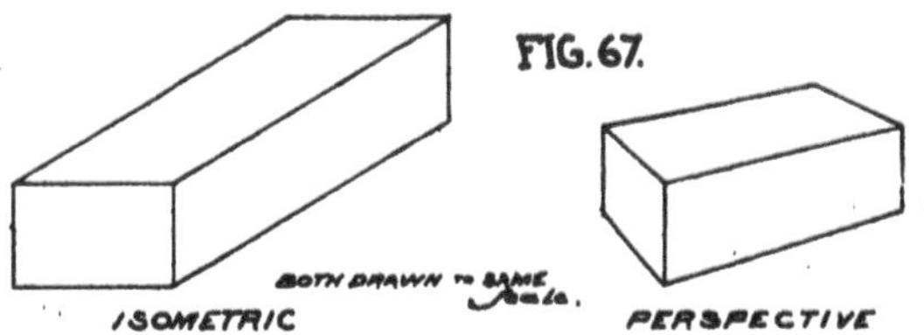

FIG. 67.

*Isometric Perspective or Isometric Projection is a branch of higher draftsmanship and not treated in this book. It will appear in an advanced book of this series.

This Chart No. 1, as presented in the regular course for beginners at Mechanics Institute, is given here as a simple example; one embracing the fundamental principles of the making of architectural plans and the reading of them. It is not a complete comprehensive and exhaustive treatment of the subject, but clearly explains the basic principles, so far as plans and elevations go (Sectional drawings will be treated elsewhere in this book).

Chart No. 1, Fig. 60, also typifies the underlying principles of constructive drawing, grouping and arrangement; a system which should be followed in the arrangement of all charts for study purposes.*

In this respect the lessons to be learned are: First: To have an object in mind before beginning the operation of making a drawing. Second: To know how to begin to draw, in such a way that all its parts or necessary views shall be so placed that their relation to each other is unmistakable; that all who have need, may read and understand. It also affords practice in simple line making, starting, stopping and joining of lines, and at same time gives a slight insight of mechanical construction with material. It should be understood, however, that all drawings cannot be started in the same manner, but the basic principle is the same in all. In other words; there must be a place for the starting and a correct way of doing it.

The Figs. 60-a-b-c, Chart 1, are practice studies covering the field above described, each representing a conventional method of "bonding" (tying-in or overlapping) of brick and the particular class to which they belong is indicated by the individual titles.

The next figure, 68, represents a simple system of laying off a sheet into panels of equal proportions for the purpose of symmetrical arrangement of as many

*Students are often embarrassed in making a start on a drawing and for such in particular a careful study of this system will prove beneficial.

separate figures as are represented by the panels drawn. It is a system employed by the author of this book in Teachers' College. Also at Atelier*-Guissart, New York City.

As with Chart No. I, this is a very simple application of right line (straight line) construction. It differs from the first, however, in that it puts geometric formula or rule into immediate practice by an application most useful to an architectural draftsman. The simple geometric problem of "dividing" a given line into proportionate parts, not necessarily uniform or equal parts, but parts in proportion one to another as may be desired.

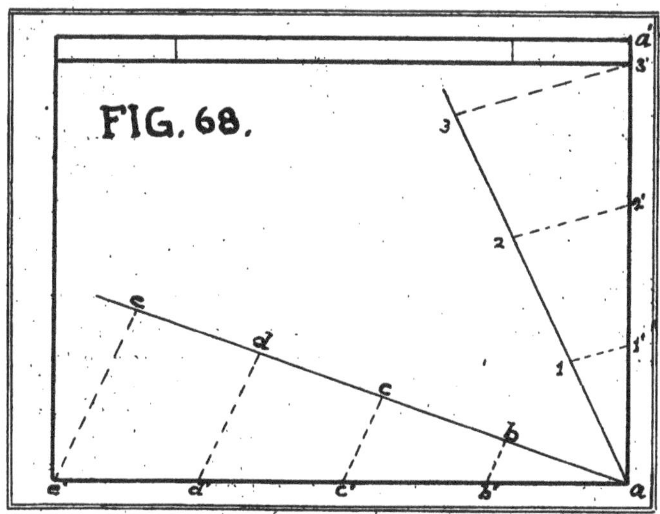

*"Atelier" means, the work-shop of an artist.

The paper used is of standard size and shape—see page 77.

The trimming lines and marginal lines are laid off in same manner shown on page 82. The result desired is the dividing of the panel formed by the innermost marginal lines, into twelve smaller panels of equal size.

We begin by drawing a line at any angle with the lower marginal (border) line beginning at the point marked "a"* (the exact angle of this line is entirely optional with the draftsman) and extending indefinitely within the bounds of the border lines.

On this line, from the point "a" as a zero mark on scale, mark off four equal spaces of any dimension, say 3 standard inches; as indicated on diagram as "b"-"c"-"d"-"e." Remove scale, and draw a light line from e to e′ (e to e prime†) which is the farthermost point on the line to be subdivided (a, the zero point, the beginning, and e′ the ending or finish) next, draw lines successively from d to d′—c to c′ and b to b′. In each case paralleling the line first drawn from e to e′.

This is accomplished as described. (See Fig. 12.) The same method is now applied for spacing the perpendicular line a-a″ (a to a second) into three equal parts, again using any measurement optionally, and resulting in the points marked 1-2-3. 3 and a″ are now united by a light line and 2 and 1 paralleled with this line to and intersecting with the perpendicular line a—a″.

From points 2′ and 1′ draw horizontal lines by aid of the T-square, stopping at the marginal line opposite. Then, reversing T-square, or (if board is imperfect) use set square in combination with T-square (See Fig. 55) and erect the perpendicular lines from

*See Fig. 68.

†"Prime" means "First", i. e., the first repetition of marking of a designated point.

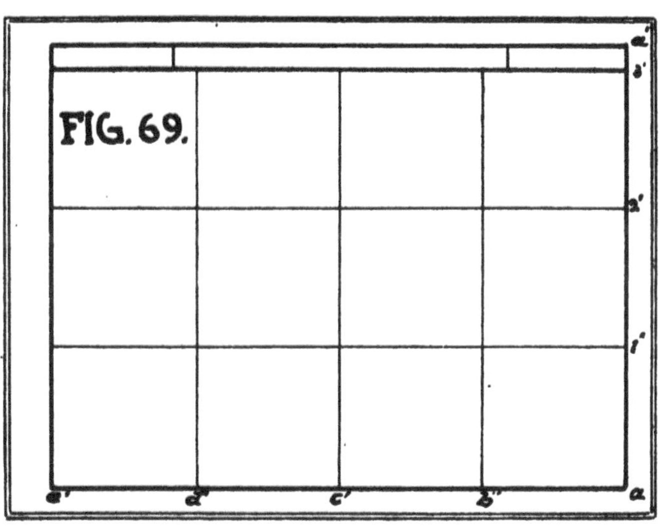

FIG. 69.

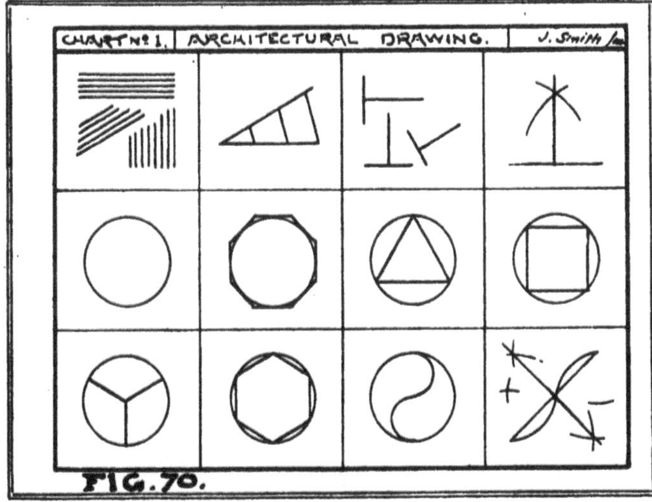

FIG. 70.

points d'—c' and b' stopping at the upper marginal line, with result as shown in Fig. 69. Twelve inner panels of equal size and form ready to receive a series of figures or forms of a classification or such as it may be desirable to group together. See Fig. 70.

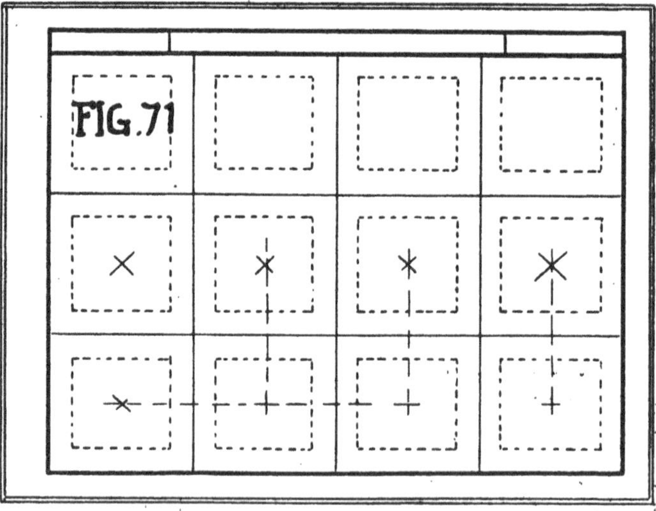

Fig. 71 shows the inner panel guide lines (dotted lines) which are to be made in lead pencil and erased after the figures are inked in.

There are other ways for producing the same result, each of which is equally simple if not equally important to the beginner and as involving principles most useful in general practice.

Time will not be squandered therefore by a little devotion to them. These panels may be laid off by the use of the Scale, which affords practice in the making of measurements; and for this purpose it may be best, if the instructor prompts the suggestion that the larger panel* be regarded as having been made at a given scale, say ¼"=1 ft. The total length of this long panel is then measured as representing so many feet and inches, and this total, mathematically divided by

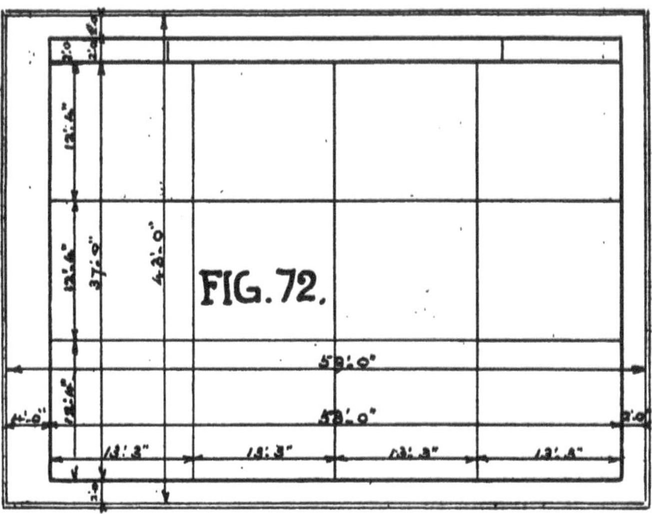

FIG. 72.

Scale ¼"=1 ft.

4 to determine the exact length of each of the smaller panels. Which in turn should be measured off into so many feet and inches, or fractions, as the mathematical calculation has demonstrated it to be.

The same process is resorted to in the laying off of the perpendicular measurements and the lines drawn as in Fig. 69.

Another method for producing the same result is

*In each case it is assumed that the marginal lines have been affixed as described on page 79.

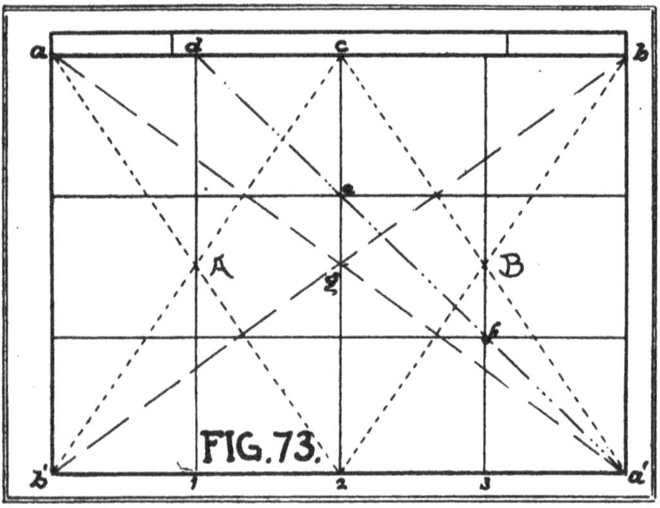

FIG. 73.

by a combination of the use of the **diagonal** line together with the problem shown in Fig. 73.

Inside of the marginal lines, draw the diagonals a,-a', and b,-b' which fixes the exact centre of panel; (See Fig. 62).

Draw the centre, perpendicular line (the perpendicular or vertical axis, see Fig. 63) terminating at points marked c and thereby forming two panels, A and B. Strike diagonal lines across both of these last formed panels, thus: a to c, b to d, and a' to d', b' to c, thus fixing the exact centre of each panel (A and B). Draw perpendicular lines through these new centres terminating at points e-e' and f-f', now: strike a diagonal line from e' to b and where this line **intersects*** the line c-d and f-f' we have points g and h;

*See Figs. 62 and 63.

draw lines horizontally through these points g and h, and the final result will be 12 equal panels as in Fig. 73. Another way, particularly useful in the

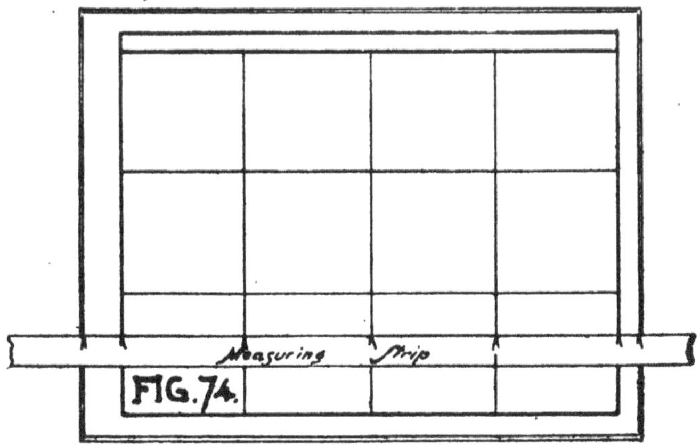

FIG. 74.

matter of time saving, is to use the "measuring strip," Fig. 74.

A fifth method is accomplished by "pricking," a means for duplication or copying but not for the original production of form. For this process, put the original on top of the paper to which the duplication is to be made, square both papers and secure them with thumb-tacks. Now, with a sharp, fine needle point* (do not use the points of dividers for this purpose, they are too coarse) make the slightest punctures possible for leaving an imprint, at each and every intersection of line successively, until every intersection has been indicated on paper beneath. When pricking is completed remove the original draw-

*Such points are provided in the handle of a ruling pen, sometimes, and it is available by unscrewing the metal part from handle.

ing by lifting the thumb tacks, one at a time, and immediately replacing it to secure the same corner of the paper beneath, without permitting its position being changed or put out of square. After the original has been released from paper beneath, examine the sheet very carefully, locate the points necessary to be connected and draw the lines, using T-square and set-square in combination when necessary. Do not use the set-square apart from the T-square in this work except for angular or oblique lines. If used

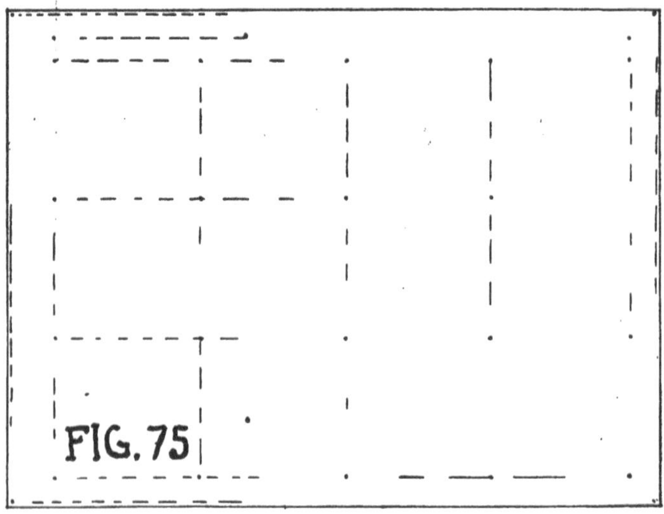

independently for horizontal or perpendicular lines the chances are against such lines being parallel where it is important they should. The process of line making by connecting of points (piercings or indentations) is continued to a completion of all lines. It is superfluous, perhaps, to say that it is absolutely necessary such work must be done in lead pencil before attempting to put the lines in ink. There is a good chance for error unless the work is very carefully done which should be safeguarded.

Centre points for circles are located, and curved lines can be reproduced by "pricking" at short intervals throughout the full length of line, curved or complexed.*

Reproduction by pricking is a delicate process if a clean drawing is desired, particularly when the drawing is on a small scale; but it has a great advantage in the saving of time, and if carefully done, accuracy

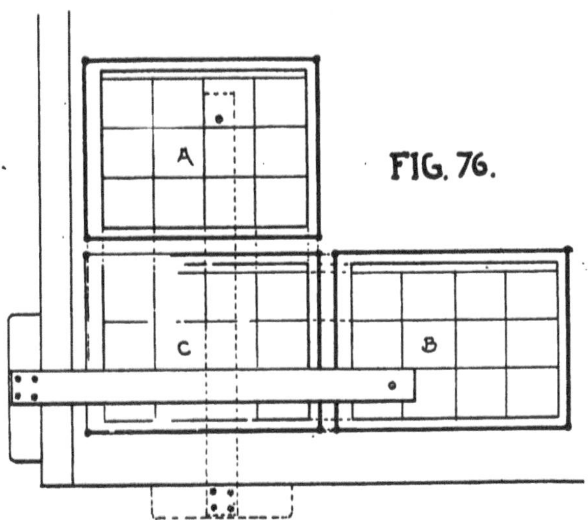

FIG. 76.

of measurement and form, fully compensates for the somewhat strenuous effort.

*This is a very ready aid to the artist, artisan or mechanic, in copying the profile lines exactly as presented, and required by the architect.

A sixth method of transferring lines and measurements is by what is known as Orthographic Projection, an exceedingly useful process, more so perhaps to the Mechanical or Technical draftsman than to the man who devotes himself to architectural drawing exclusively. Nevertheless, to him it has a great value, therefore is much used by him

Orthographic Projection is a method of accomplishing same results already described in the matter of transference of lines; differing from them, however, in that it depends exclusively on transference being made, by "**projection**" of lines drawn at once from the original to the new position as required (see Fig. 76).

This is not only an exceedingly useful method but one absolutely indispensable to the architectural draftsman. By its agency, results may be obtained which are impossible of accomplishment by any other method. Orthographic projection is indispensable to a draftsman in any and all the mechanical or technical pursuits.

The uses to which orthographic projection may be put are numerous, but for the present needs of the architectural student the plates and charts that follow will suffice to illustrate its usefulness.

IV.

GEOMETRIC FORMULA.

Geometric formula are things not to be despised by the architectural draftsman. Neither is it necessary to skillfulness in this particular line of draftsmanship, to know all there is to be known about the exact mathematical relation of one angle to another, or the properties of figures in space geometrically considered in all its intricacies of detail. He should, however, have some slight understanding of common elementary and practical geometry. If he is not qualified to "deduct the properties of figures in space from their defining conditions by means of assumed properties of space" he should at leâst, know the common value and ordinary use of the simple forms of geometric problems and have some conception of the application of them to practical uses for producing practical results. If he needs an Ellipse he should have a method in mind or at least at hand, for producing one of the characters needed. If he needs a geometrically correct Cyma-recta or a Cyma-reversa he should be equal to the task of producing it.

We have already in the pages of this book had occasion frequently to refer to geometric application and the student will have use for others, therefore the following examples are incorporated to illustrate their real value in practical application to the actual needs of the architectural draftsman.

Right Lines—Chart No. II: Scale, One Normal Inch equalling one Foot.

Is a study in "Right Lines" (straight lines).

Draw all marginal lines and trimming lines first (in lead-pencil). See Figs. 51-52.

Fig. 77 deals with horizontal and perpendicular lines only.

The object is to teach exactness of spacing by measurement and symmetrical arrangement of the subject. Fig. 78 shows the method of procedure or the way to do the work. First: Find the centre of paper by diagonal lines. Draw **Centre line** perpendicular. Draw a line 1′-0″ below the top marginal line and parallel with it: Measure off 3′-0″ each way from centre line and draw a perpendicular line at each extremity: Space off the perpendiculars by alternate spacings of 1′-8″ and 6″: Draw horizontal lines from these points of measurement thereby producing panels 1′-8″ wide by 6′-0″ and 6″ apart.

All detail spacings are 2″ wide: Lay-off three of them at the top and two at the bottom of each panel.

Fill in all intermediate lines as shown in Fig. 77.

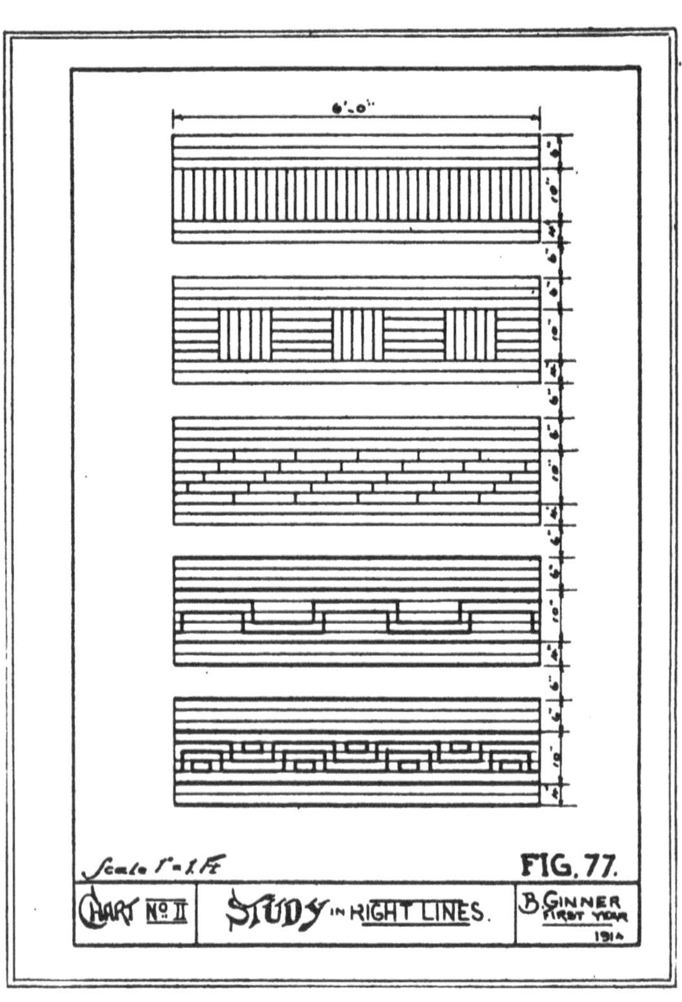
6'-0"
Scale 1" = 1 Ft
FIG. 77.
CHART No. II
STUDY IN RIGHT LINES.
B. GINNER
FIRST YEAR
1914

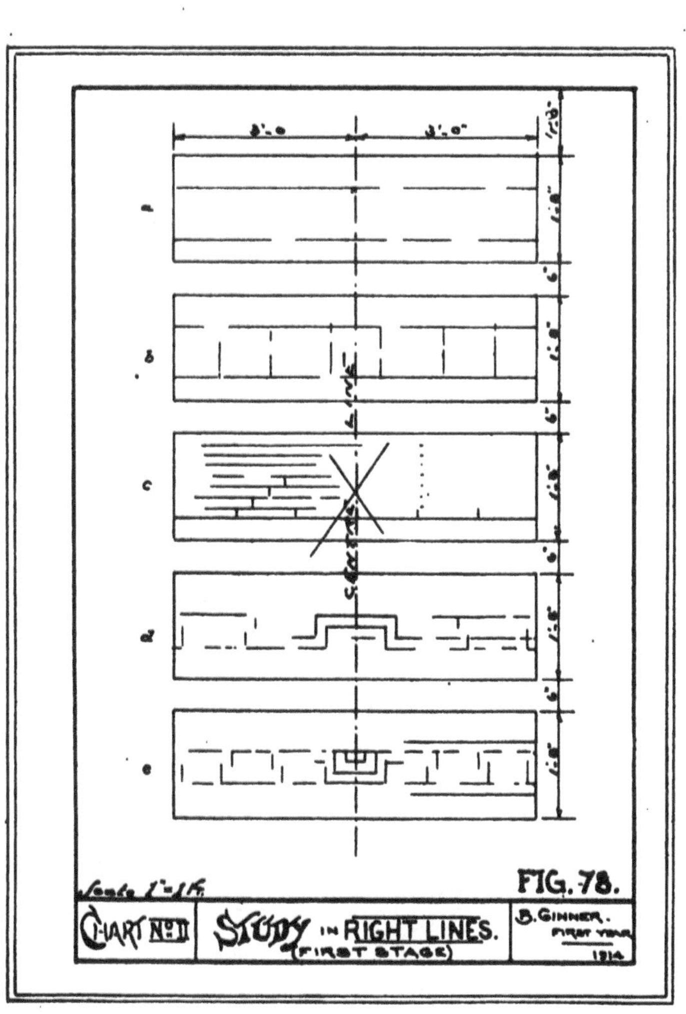

3'-0"
3'-0"
a
b
c
d
e
CENTRE LINE
1'-6"
6"
Scale 1"=1 Ft.
FIG. 78.
CHART No II
STUDY IN RIGHT LINES.
(FIRST STAGE)
B. GINNER.
FIRST YEAR
1914

6'-0"
Scale 1" = 1 Ft.
FIG. 79.
CHART No III
STUDY IN RIGHT LINES.
B. GINNER
FIRST YEAR
1914

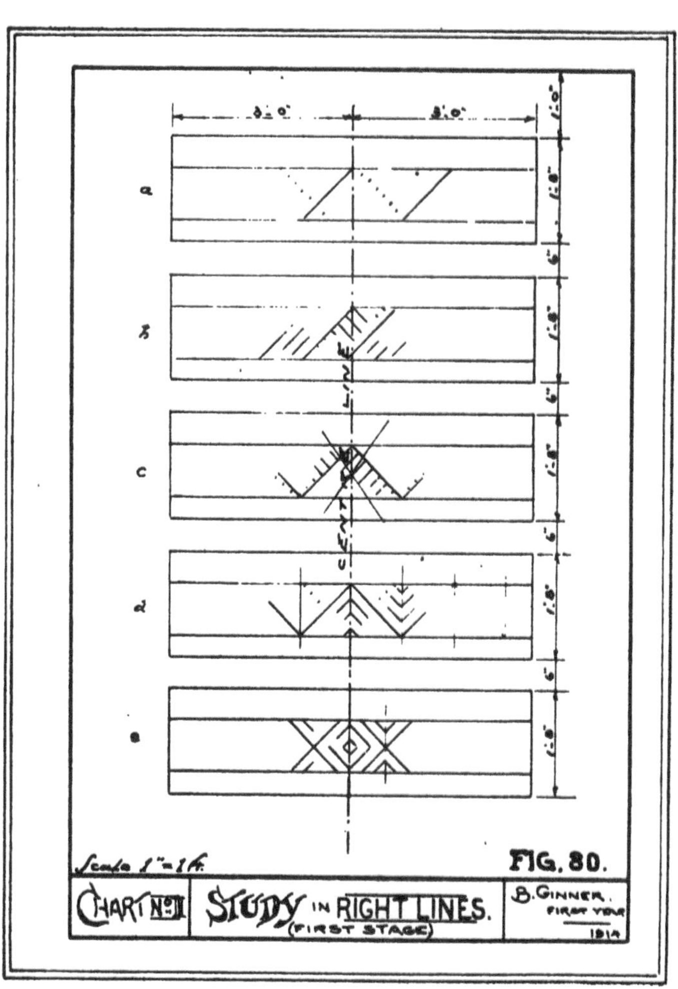

3'-0"
3'-0"
1'-0"
a
1'-8"
6"
b
1'-8"
6"
c
1'-8"
6"
d
1'-8"
6"
e
1'-8"
CENTRE LINE
Scale 1" = 1 ft.
FIG. 80.
CHART No. II
STUDY IN RIGHT LINES.
(FIRST STAGE)
B. GINNER.
FIRST YEAR
1914

Fig. 79: A similar study of horizontal lines with the addition of oblique lines, diagonal lines.

Block out panels in same manner as in Fig. 78. But put in constructional lines as shown in Fig. 80.

Fill in middle spacings with diagonal lines at an angle of 45°. Use the 45° set-square for this purpose.

The **dots** show how measurements are to be laid off —the direction in which they are measured—a—b—c— are made with diagonal lines only, d—e, introduces the use of centre-lines in constructive design.

Inking-in.—For the manner of loading or charging the pen with ink: See page 50.

Set the pen for fine lines, not to the limit of fineness, but a medium fine line.

Begin at the top, the top line of the problem marked a—and follow with all horizontal lines from top to bottom.

Draw all lines from left to right.

When horizontal lines are finished put in the verticals, that is, all lines which are **perpendicular** to the horizontal lines.

Draw all vertical lines from bottom to top, i. e.— from left to right, turning the person to the right if necessary, to facilitate doing this. Stand up while making such lines if you must. It is not always convenient to make them while sitting still.

After all horizontal and all vertical lines are done, put in the marginal lines. And for this purpose set the pen to a gage which will produce a line in marked contrast with the lines of the drawing, say about three times the thickness of such lines.

Put in the top horizontal line and follow with those at the bottom of sheet. **Wait until ink is dry**—then

Put in the vertical marginal lines—The one to the left first.

Draw from bottom up—left to right.

Change setting of pen to a **fine** line (quite fine).

Put in the "**trimming lines,**" See Fig. 51.

These trimming lines should be carefully drawn but it is not necessary to stop exactly at the points of intersection, the lines may with consistency cross in this instance.

Do all lettering and marking of figures, measurement lines, Title, Scale, etc.

Clean the entire surface of paper with a **sponge rubber** (paper cleaner). Use a harder rubber to remove pencil marks if necessary. If accident has occurred to lines by overlapping or otherwise, remove the defect with the point of a knife, finishing with a soft rubber. If a spot of ink has gotten on paper; remove the bulk of it by carefully going over the surface with sharp **edge** of knife blade, then apply the rubber, according to the need, sand rubber if necessary, but it must be used gently and by persistent rubbing. Finish with a soft rubber.

The chart is now finished and ready to be trimmed.

Do not trim with knife on drawing-board.

Do not use T-square blade as a straight edge for trimming with a knife. It is far better to use scissors or shears.

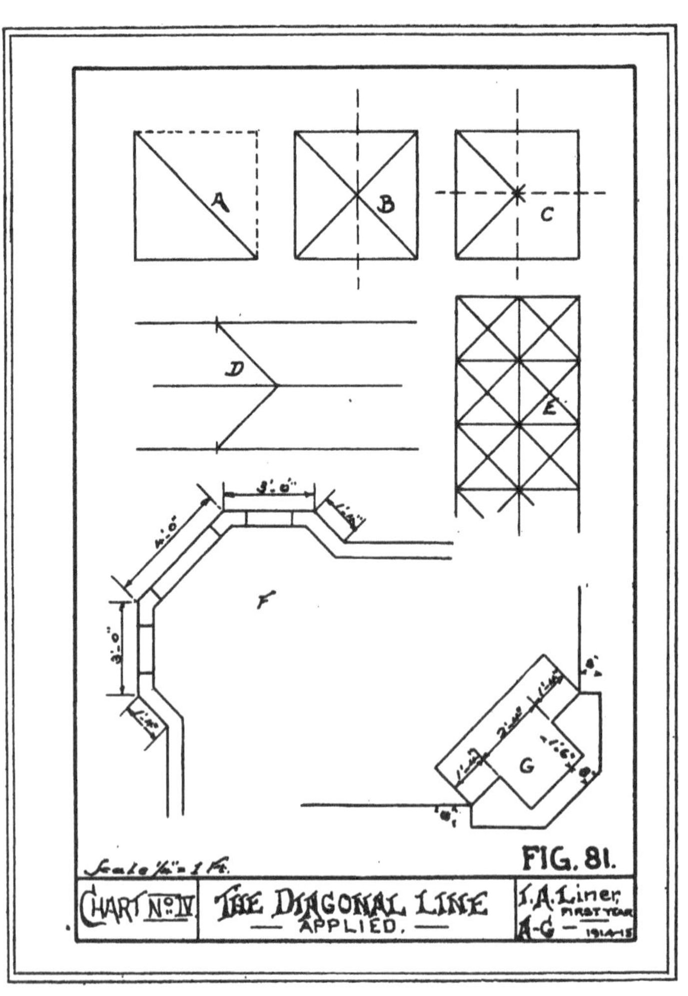

FIG. 81.

A
B
C
D
E
F
G
centre line
WALL
WALL
CHART No. IV
THE DIAGONAL LINE
APPLIED.
I.A. Liner,
FIRST YEAR
A.G.
1914-15

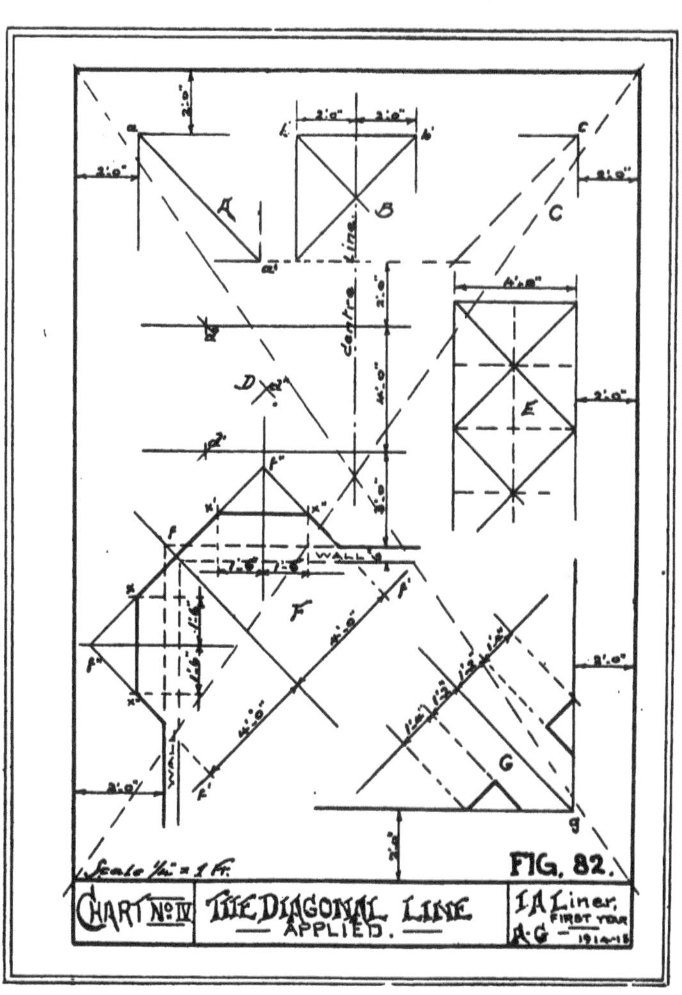

FIG. 82.

V.

APPLICATION OF RIGHT LINES AND OBLIQUE LINES.

Chart IV. Figs. 81-82, Scale ¼"=1 foot.

Draw trimming lines and marginal lines in lead pencil.

Locate the guide lines fixing the limit of space to be occupied by the subject. See Fig. 82.

Draw A—which represents an angle of 45°, one-half a perfect square (See Fig. 83). The dotted lines

FIG. 83.

complete the square. The oblique line a—a' is the **diagonal line,** or hypotenuse.

Draw B—measuring from the center line both ways.

From points b—b' draw diagonal lines, indefinitely.

Draw perpendiculars from b—b' down, until they strike the diagonals.

Complete the square by drawing the bottom line.

Draw a complete square at C—and find the centre by drawing two lines at an angle of 45°.

D—Draw two horizontal lines 4 feet apart and 2' 0" below square B.

Fix two points, d—d' anywhere on the lines provided one is directly above the other.

From these two points d—d′, draw diagonal lines and they will cross exactly midway between the two lines; d″ is therefore a point through which a line drawn will divide the space between the lines first drawn into two equal spacings.

E—Construct a square of 4′ 0″ and by the use of diagonal lines and centre lines, construct a number of smaller squares.

F—Draw the horizontal and perpendicular lines, (representing the walls of a frame house) out to the square corner f..

From f draw a diagonal line at 45°.

Draw a line f′—f′ at right angles, or perpendicular to line f and at any distance from the corner, either inside or outside the walls. (It is drawn on the inside on the chart for convenience).

Measure the width of the corner bay-window on the line last drawn—4′ 0″ each way from line f, which now also becomes a **centre line.**

Extend these measurements to points f″ which is 3′ 6″ beyond the outside face of walls.

Draw f″—f″ together and mark off 2′ 0″ each way from the centre line f and so fixing the points x—x′. Measure the points x″—x″, 1′ 4″ from face of walls.

Connect x—x″ and x′—x″ by a vertical and a horizontal line and an octagonal bay is outlined on the exact corner of the building.

Draw the inside lines, 6″ from the outline already drawn, to represent the thickness of walls to bay.

Fix the windows by short lines 6″ from the inner angles each way.

G—Represents an inner angle of a room into which it is desired to draw a fire-place.

Proceed as in the previous example by establishing two lines at right angles (90°).

From corner g, draw a diagonal line (45°).

CHART No V.
Prob. 1.
Prob. 2.
(TEN SPACES - 16" ON CENTRES)
Prob. 3.
Prob. 4.
Prob. 5.

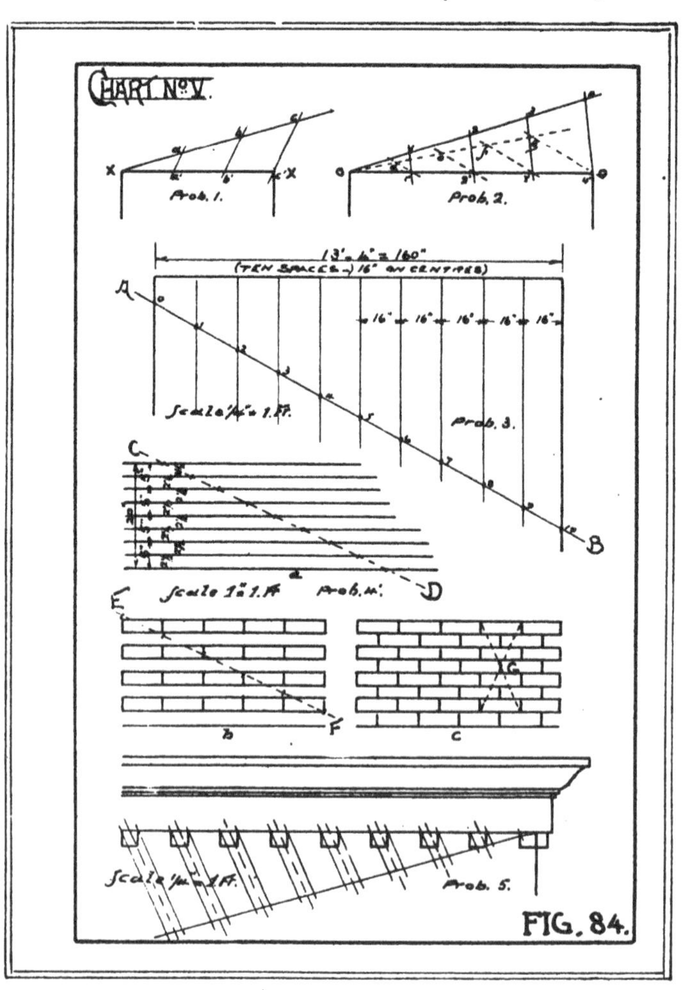

FIG. 84.

Draw a measuring line at right angles to the diagonal line, anywhere on that line.

Mark off measurements and proceed as in previous example.

Chart V. Fig. 84—Problem 1.

To divide a given line into any number of **proportionate** parts (equal or unequal).

x—x represents the head of a door or window opening as the given line.

From x draw a line at any angle and of any length.

Mark on this line, three spaces of desired proportions (they are equal in this example).

Mark these points, a—b—c.

Draw c and c′ by a light line and from b and a draw similar lines **parallel** to it. Where they each cut the given line they will divide it into the same number of spaces as the angular line and in exact proportion.

Problem 2 is the same thing but showing two different angular lines and two entirely different proportions of measurements which when projected, each verifies the correctness of the other.

Problem 3 shows the method applied for the purpose of spacing floor beams or similar parts, with a minimum of labor.

The distance to be spaced (the given line) is here represented as being 13′-4″, which when reduced to inches equals 160.

Divide 160 by 16 which represents the inches that each space is to cover which results in **ten spaces.**

It therefore becomes necessary to lay off ten spaces of equal measurement.

Having drawn the two side lines which fixes the space to be divided, lay the Scale across, with the zero mark (0) resting on side line at A—and the 10 foot mark, at any scale, resting on side line at B.

The side lines A—B being parallel, all lines of projection must be parallel with them, which when drawn results in the equal spacings and nine lines representing floor beams 16″ on centres.

The side lines A—B, represent walls.

Problem 4 is the same thing laying off a number of courses of brick in a given height, say 20″, each brick including mortar joints measuring 2½″, or two courses to 5″.

b—c, Problem 4, shows the vertical spacing for the length of the bricks. The measurements on line E—F, fixes alternate courses, while the diagonal lines fixes a starting point from which to measure the filling in courses of brick. The measuring for this can be done by aid of a measuring strip. See Fig. 44.

Problem 5. The same process for laying off **Modillions** or **Dentals** to a cornice. It will be observed that here we have two separate sets of measurements proportionately projected.

The same result may be reached by projecting one series of measurements only (see dotted lines), and using such as centre lines from which the width of modillions is measured.

It should be observed that in this instance the contact of the angular line with the horizontal, must be at the centre of the first, or corner modillion. (In the problem, the first space has been increased to compensate for the needed precaution.)

A
B
D
C
E
Scale 1" = 1 Ft.
CHART No.
THE CIRCLE
A. ROUNDER
— FIRST YEAR
1914-15
FIG. 85.

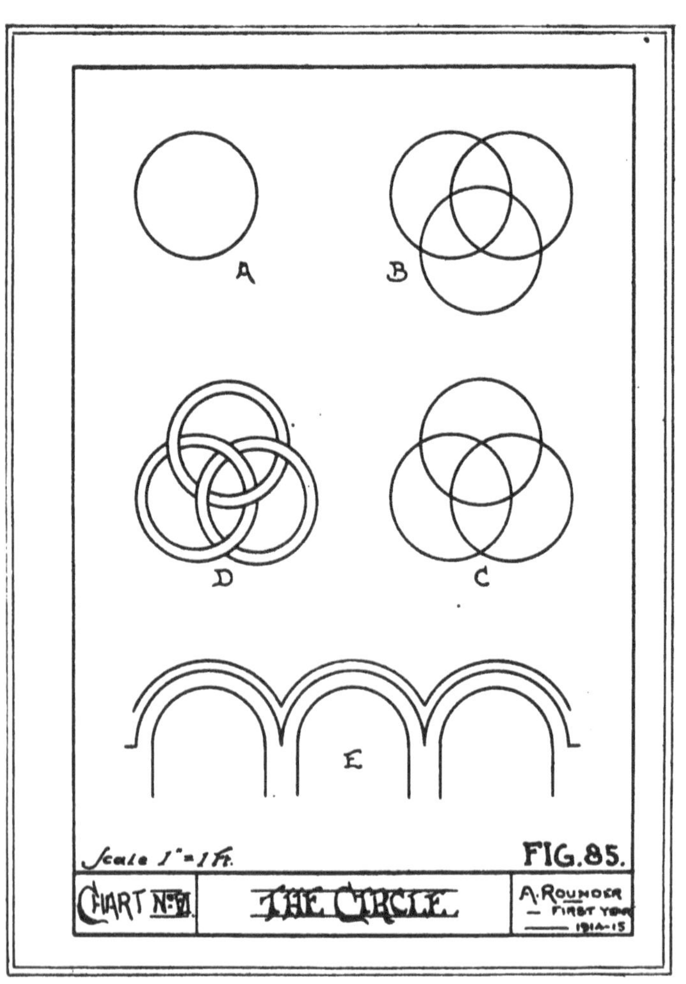

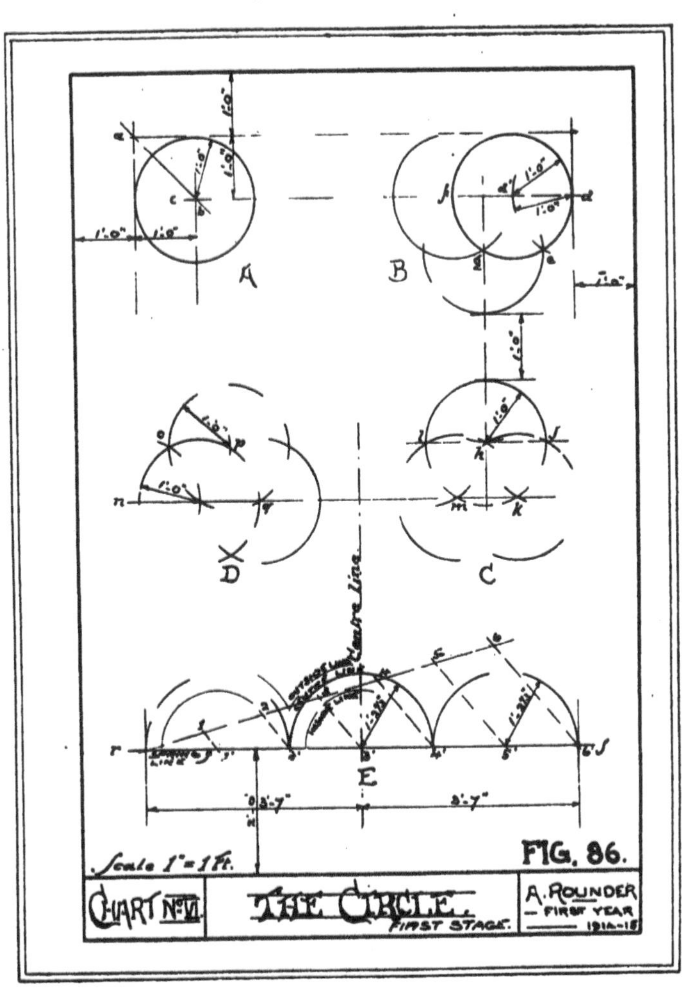
A
B
C
D
E
Centre Line
Scale 1" = 1 Ft.
FIG. 86.
CHART No VI
THE CIRCLE.
FIRST STAGE.
A. ROUNDER
FIRST YEAR
1914-15

VI.

THE CIRCLE.

Chart VI. Figs. 85-86. Scale 1 inch=1 foot.

The Circle and simple application of it. The circle is used in many ways and for many purposes,

Draw top and side lines, guide lines, Fig. 86.

Construct circle A, by aid of the diagonal line a-b. The centre c, being equal distant from both top and side guide lines which fixes the diameter by establishing the radial point, the centre, the **radius** thereby becoming 1′ 0″.

From centre c draw a dotted line, horizontally to d, passing through f.

Fix centre of the circle, d′, diagram B, by laying off the radius, 1′-0″, from point d, by aid of compass.

With same radius, from point d, lay off point e, and from f lay off g. The measurement from e to g would confirm the correctness of the point, f and g are the centres from which the additional circles are swept.

The figure thus made is a **Trefoil,** a three-foil figure; The three curved lines, arcs of circles which make the outline, are called "**foils.**" The points of intersection between foils are "**cusps.**"

C—Is a repetition of the last figure but reversed or inverted.

The centre h, becoming the counterpart of g, m represents f, and k duplicates d′.

A careful study of the figure will reveal the method.

D—The same thing transferred to a new position and embellished as three linking rings. (Be careful about the over-running and the underlaying lines.)

E—A series of three arches equally spaced within a given distance, say, 7′-2″.

Locate the Spring-line and the Centre-line.

Measure the total width, 7′-2″, from centre line by two factors, 3′-7″ each.

Find the centres of the three arches by dividing the length of spring line into **six** equal parts.

The alternate points marked 1′-3′-5′, being the required centres.

Spring the semi-circles with a compass, and the lines so produced will represent the centre lines of the finished arches. See Fig. 85, diagram E.

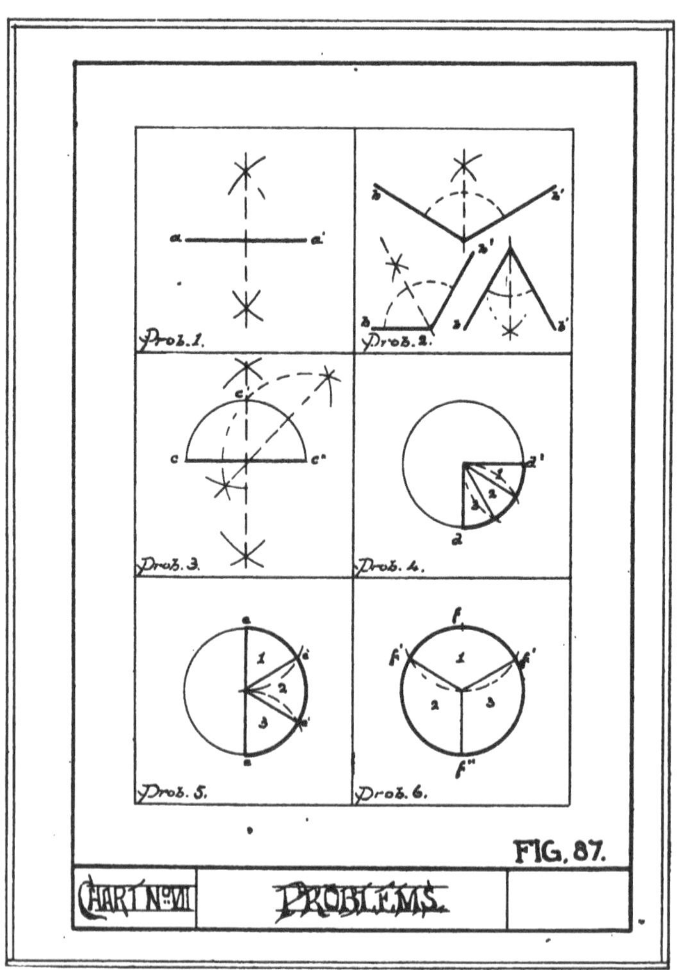

FIG. 87.

VII.

BI-SECTION AND TRI-SECTION.

Chart VII. Fig. 87 (Not drawn to scale).

Problem 1—A simple bi-section of a line, a "Right-line."

The line a-a′ may be of any length.

From point a, as a centre point, strike an arc of a circle both above and below the horizontal line.

With the same radius, strike similar arcs from the point a′, and where the arcs cross each other we have two points which if connected by a straight line will divide the line a-a′ into exactly two equal parts.

This is called "Bi-secting a line."

Problem 2—Strike a small arc, any radius, using the union or "apex" of the angular lines as a centre. And with the same radius, or any radius equal to more than one-half the length of arc, strike two minor arcs, midway in the angular space.

Draw the point so created and the apex of angular lines together, and the angular space will thus have been divided into two equal parts.

Problem 3—Is the bi-secting of an arc of a circle.

In the example, the curved line, c-c′-c″, represents a semi-circle. The bi-section of which is accomplished in same manner as that of a straight line, by two sweeps somewhat more than one-half the line to be bi-sected.

In this problem a second example is shown, wherein a lesser arc, that is, c′-c″ is bi-sected in the same way. (There is no straight line in connection with this lesser arc to confuse matters.)

Problem 4—**Tri-Section.**

The possibility of tri-secting space and lines is extremely limited.

Three illustrations only, of possibilities of accomplishing this result are here shown.

Problem 4—Is the tri-section of a quarter circle, a "Quadrant."

It is accomplished by using one-half the diameter as a sweep, and the two extreme points of the arc or quarter circle d-d′, as centres.

Draw the points of intersection and the centre point together and we have three equal spaces as marked, 1-2-3.

Problem 5—Tri-section of a Semi-circle.

Take one-half the diameter as a radius and with it sweep the semi-circle from the extremities e-e, and with the same radius, using e-e as centres, draw two arcs cutting the semi-circle in e′-e′.

Draw lines from e′-e′ to the centre of circle and the three equal parts of a semi-circle will have been created as shown by, 1-2-3.

Problem 6—Tri-section of a Circle.

Take the radius of the circle for a sweep.

Take a point on the circle, anywhere; as a centre and as indicated at f.

Strike an arc which will cut the circle at two points, as at f′-f′.

Draw lines from f′-f′ to the centre of circle and a space equal to one-third the area of the circle will have been thus confined.

The remaining two-thirds are determined by dropping a perpendicular line from the centre point, or by laying off the distance between f′-f′, on the circle resulting in f″.

Draw this point f″ and the centre point together and the result will be the circle divided into three equal parts as shown at 1-2-3.

[By careful observation the student will learn that these same tri-sections can be accomplished by the use of the 30-60-90 triangle in conjunction with a T-square.]

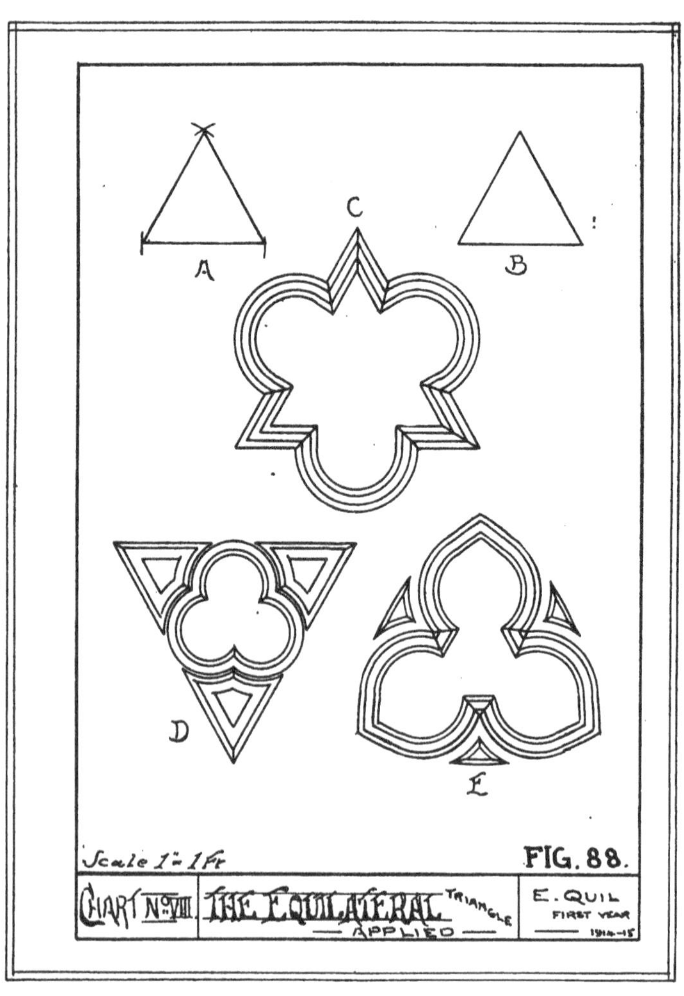
A
B
C
D
E
Scale 1" = 1 Ft
FIG. 88.
CHART No. VIII
THE EQUILATERAL TRIANGLE
— APPLIED —
E. QUIL
FIRST YEAR
1914-15

A
B
C
D
E
Scale 1" = 1 Ft
FIG. 88.
CHART No. VIII.
THE EQUILATERAL TRIANGLE
APPLIED
E. QUIL
FIRST YEAR
1914-15

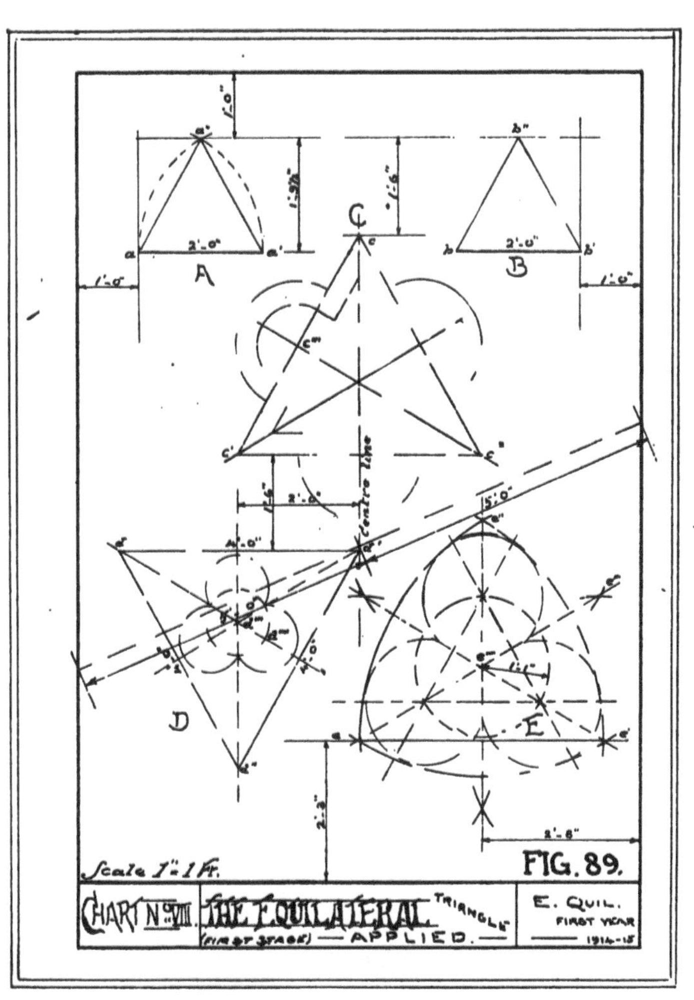
A
B
C
D
E
Centre line
Scale 1" = 1 Ft.
FIG. 89.
CHART No. VIII
THE EQUILATERAL TRIANGLE
(FIRST STAGE) — APPLIED. —
E. QUIL.
FIRST YEAR
1914-15

VIII.

THE EQUILATERAL TRIANGLE.

The Circle—Bi-section and Tri-section Applied.

Chart VIII—Figs. 88-89. Scale 1″=1 Ft.

Find the centre line as shown by two measurements of 5′ 0″ each. A—Represents an Equilateral-triangle geometrically constructed on a given line-a **"base line."**

Take the length of the line by compass and with a, as a centre strike an arc above the line.

With same radius, strike another arc from a′ and inter-secting the arc first drawn.

This point of inter-section, a″, and points a and a′ united by lines, produces an equilateral-triangle.

A three-sided figure with the sides of equal length.

B—The same figure accomplished by the aid of a 30-60-90 triangle (set-square), because of the fact that a 30-60-90 triangle is just one-half an equilateral. (See Fig. 90).

C—An Equilateral **Tre-foil.**

Bi-sect the three lines c to c′—c′ to c″ and c″ to c. It may be done by aid of a 30° angle as shown at c″″, or, the bi-section may be done with the compass.

These points of bi-section constitute the centre points from which the foiliating arcs are swept.

The **foils** may be of any size and of any sweep to the limit of uniting as a true circle.

D—A Tre-foil within the circumference of a **right line** equilateral.

The extreme measurement of radius is fixed by the right-lines.

E—Another form: Centres being fixed through the bi-section of right-lines and arcs of circles.

There are three forms of equilaterals in this figure, one with right-lines and two with curved lines.

-A-
-C-
-E-
-B-
-D-
-F-
-G-
-H-
J-
-K
DETAILS-FULL SIZE.
CHART No IX
A STUDY IN CYMA
AND CYMA-REVERSA
OGEES
A. BENDER
— FIRST YEAR
FIG. 91.

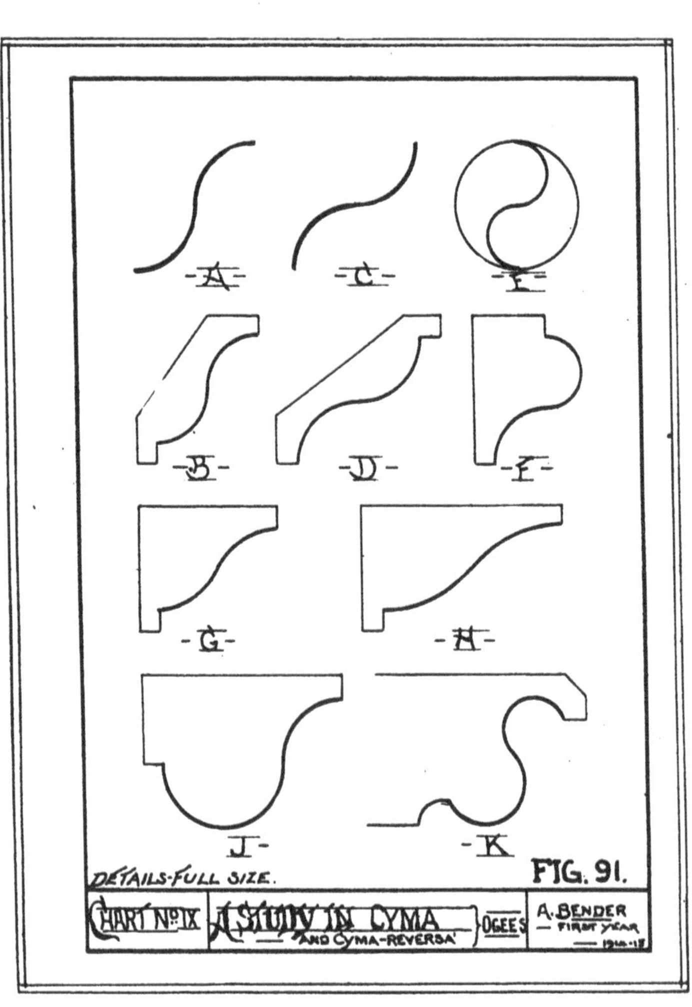

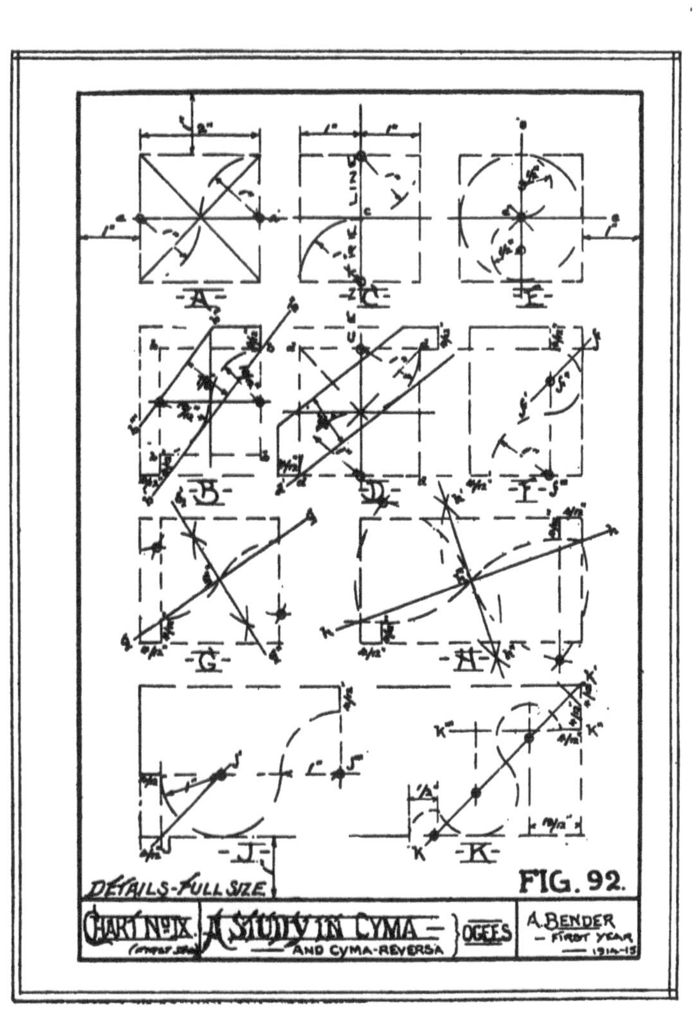
DETAILS-FULL SIZE
FIG. 92.
CHART No IX.
A STUDY IN CYMA
AND CYMA-REVERSA
OGEES
A. BENDER
- FIRST YEAR
1914-15
A
B
C
D
E
F
G
H
J
K

IX.

The CYMA-RECTA and CYMA-REVERSA, ("OGEES")

Chart IX. Figs. 91—92. Scale: Full-size (Standard Measurement).

A—Is a simple Cyma-recta.

Construct a square, 2"x2", one inch from top and the same distance from side margins.

Find the centre by diagonal lines.

Through this centre draw a horizontal line, the contact of which with the side lines of the square, will constitute centres at a, and a'.

From these centres, sweep two arcs, one in each direction and uniting at the centre and producing a form resembling an S.

This is a Cyma-recta.

C—Make a similar square and by use of centre lines establish similar construction, except that the centre points will be at the top and bottom of square instead of at the sides .

The result will be a similar S form reversed or inverted.

This is a Cyma-reversa. A reversed Cyma.

B—Is an application of the cyma to a moulding of wood, a form known as a "Crown-mould." Fig. 92 shows the method of construction.

It will be noted that the thickness of material from which the moulding is cut, is ⅞ of an inch, as shown by the lines b'—b" and b'"—b"".

D—A Crown-mould of the cyma-reversa type. The principles of construction are as have been described in B and C.

E—Is an exaggerated type of either a cyma or a cyma-reversa. It is inscribed within a circle with the centres of the arcs which compose the S on the vertical axes of the circle, and midway between the common centre and the periphery (out-line) of circle.

F—An application of E, modified as to the lower member and the addition of a "Quirk," the small flat member above the upper curve.

G and H—Modifications of the cyma-recta, in which the centres for sweeping the arcs are found by aid of right-lines g-g and h-h. These lines are drawn touching the points which represent the extremities of the compound curves.

Bi-sect these lines from the extreme points.

Take one-half of the bi-sected line as a radius and sweep two arcs, one from either end of the half line. The intersection of the two arcs will be the centre from which the arcs must be swept.

The principle is the same in both examples, G and H. J and K show other variations.

The student should, by this time, be able to solve their construction, and, that he may learn somewhat by experience, he is now left to his own resources.

All Cymas and Cyma-reversas are also called

Ogees—Chart X. Figs. 93-94. Scale (two of them) as marked.

These charts expand on the use and application of Ogee curves. A and B are types where the curves are united by right lines, straight lines, and elongating the ogees.

To find the centres for arcs which will be drawn tangent to two fixed lines, the method for bi-secting angles is brought into use.

It must be observed that both curves (in each ogee separately) are identical in length and radius. To illustrate: The radius b-b'''' is repeated in measure-

A
B
C
D
E
F
DETAILS FULL SIZE
G
H
CHART No. X
OGEE CURVES IN USE
O. GEE.
— FIRST YEAR
1914-15

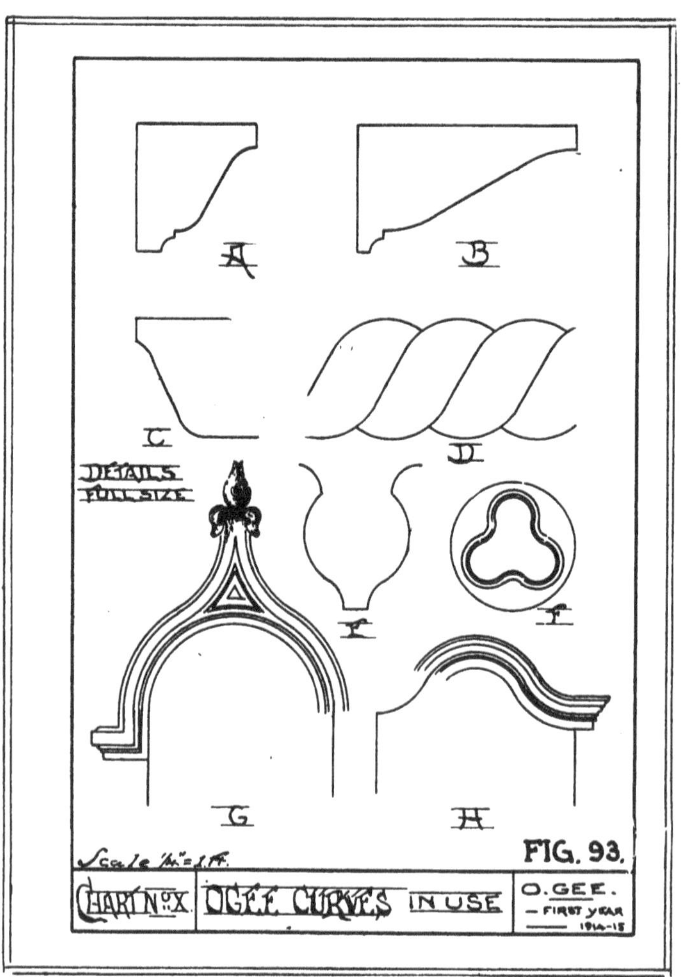

FIG. 93.

A
B
C
D
E
F
G
H
DETAILS
FULL SIZE
SPRING LINE
CHART No. X
FIRST SERIES
OGEE CURVES IN USE
O. GEE.
FIRST YEAR
1914-15

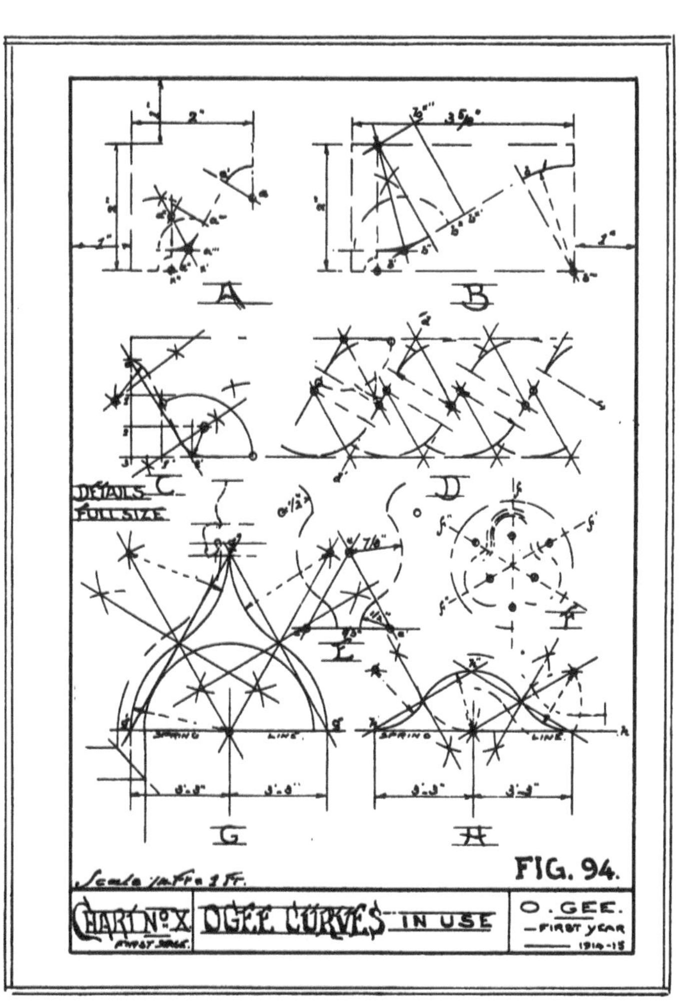

FIG. 94.

ment in line bx′-bx″ and projected to centre line (which is found through bi-section of angles) the line of projection being parallel with b-b′, the straight line of the cyma.

C—The same problem of elongated cyma, but reversed in position and proportioned on a basis of 3 parts to 2 parts.

(A further study for the student.)

D—The "Rope moulding," a series of cymas connected.

Draw the horizontal lines fixing the height, or rather the thickness of rope.

Draw the oblique lines at a spacing desired. (They are 1″ in the diagram.)

Centre lines are found through bi-section of angles, and the **centres** are fixed by spacing of oblique lines or rather by the distance between these oblique lines.

E—A "Roll and Fillet moulding."

The **fillet** is the flat member at the bottom.

The **roll** is the large sweep. The shorter sweeps are "**coves**," there are four of them.

F—The Circle—Ogee and Equilateral-triangle combined in the formation of a "Ball-Flower." An ornament much used in Gothic design.

The lines on which the centres are located are drawn with a 30° angle.

G—Is a Gothic Arch modified by a Roman **soffit** (the under side of arch). Here we have a right and a left cyma-reversa; as "extrados," or outermost contour, and a semi-circular "Intrados,"* soffit, or innermost contour.

It is drawn on the centre line principle, with a width

*The terms "Intrados" and "Extrados" applies to this and all other forms of arches.

of 6′-6″, and the spring line of same length constitutes a base line for an equilateral triangle.

The lines or planes of this equilateral triangle are bi-sected, centres found, and arcs swept as in previous examples of cyma drawing.

H—Is a type of flat ogee arch, a Bell-Arch, its flatness is fixed by angles of 30° which are first drawn from the spring line at the extreme points of the "span" (length). The arcs are produced through bi-section and projection as already described.

Measurements for Risers
Measurements for TREADS
13'-4"
12'-0"
ELEVATION.
OR SECTION.
PLAN.
Scale ½" = 1 Ft.
CHART No. XI
A STAIR-CASE.
— LAYOUT. —
A. STRAIGHTRUN.
FIRST YEAR.
M. T.
1914

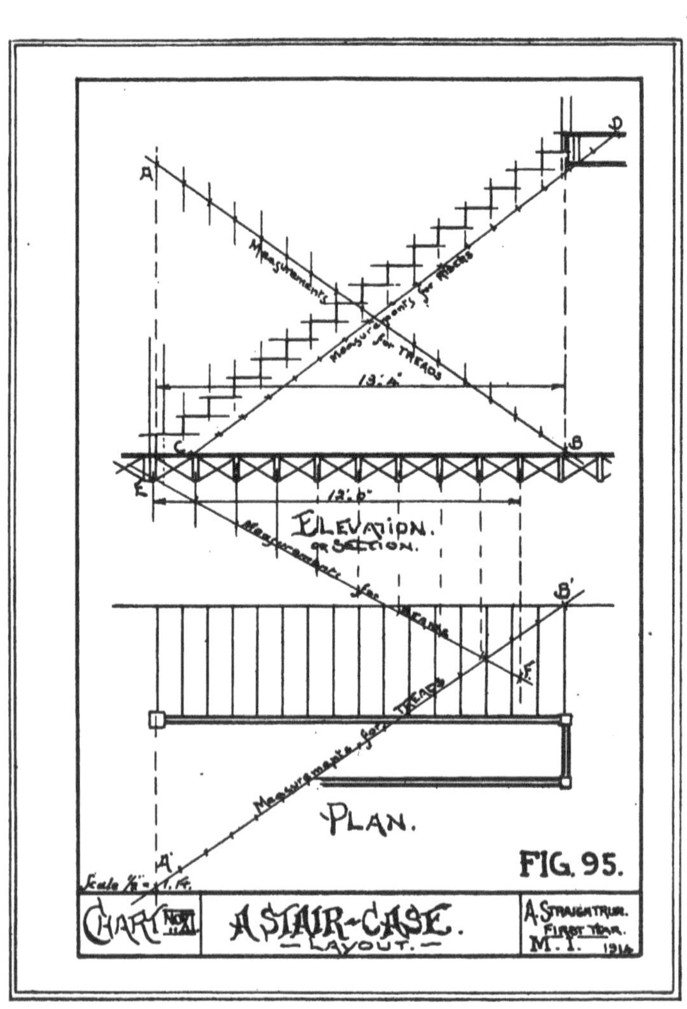

FIG. 95.

X.

GEOMETRIC APPLICATION.

Chart XI. Fig. 95. Scale ½"=1 Ft.

A Stair-case Lay-out: PLAN and ELEVATION (or Sectional view).

Both views are fully laid out by the geometric formula for dividing a given line into proportionate parts.

We will give first attention to the Sectional view, or as it may be, an **elevation.**

The first thing to do is to take the total height from floor to floor (the levels at which the stairs begin and end), in feet and inches. Mathematically reduce these feet and inches to inches, and divide by the approximate or desired height of **riser** (the upward measurement of the step). The dividend will determine the closest possible approach to desired height for each riser, as well as the number of risers to be accommodated, or necessary in the given height from floor to floor. The number of risers being fixed, regulates the number of **treads** also (treads are the flat, horizontal measurement of steps) which will be one less than the number of risers.

The top-most **tread** is actually the upper floor level consequently its width is indeterminable. These calculations having been made, it becomes a simple matter to apply the Scale to the laying off of the necessary parts. Use any scale that will fit the space, by placing the zero mark (0) at one extremity, while the figure representing as many feet as are parts desired rests at the other extremity. It is not necessary to draw a line, but mere points can be made on paper with the point of lead pencil by using the edge of scale as a straight edge, or guide provided the points so made are on an alignment close to the edge of scale.

It will be noticed there are two sets of such markings, one for treads and one for risers, and since the number of risers possible was determined by the total height from floor to floor, even so is it necessary to fix total length required for the "**run**" of the stairs, by the actual number of treads which the calculation has proven necessary; therefore it becomes imperative that we must multiply the number of treads fixed upon by the width of step, from riser to riser, exclusive of nosings. The ordinary or average measurement for this, in ordinary houses, is 10". (The overlapping "**nosing**" providing for ample rest for the foot.) According to the problem in hand the necessary treads combined will require a full run of 13′ 4", therefore the spacing must be made within two vertical lines 13′ 4" apart. The markings for both risers and treads now being laid off it becomes necessary to project one set of lines horizontally and the other set vertically and the intersecting lines thus projected will form the desired treads and risers.

In laying off the Plan, the run only of treads is taken into consideration and measurements laid off accordingly.

"Head-room" to a "stair well" is not considered in this problem. The risers are as near 7" as is possible, the total height being 10′ 0" or 120".

The floor beams beneath the stairs are placed 16" from centres. On the floor line lay off a total measurement which will subdivide equally by 16 (in the example we have taken 12′ 0"). From point at E, strike a line at any angle and measure as many parts (at any

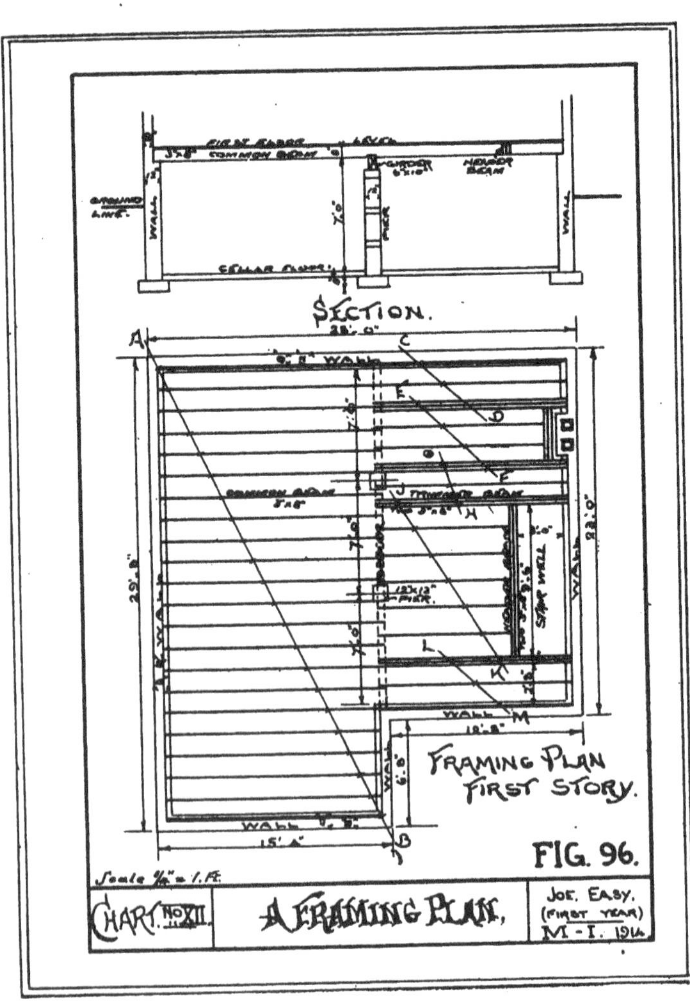
SECTION.
FRAMING PLAN
FIRST STORY.
FIG. 96.
CHART NO XII.
A FRAMING PLAN.
JOE. EASY.
(FIRST YEAR)
M-I. 1914
WALL
PIER
CELLAR FLOOR
GROUND LINE
HEADER BEAM
COMMON BEAM
STAIR WELL
12"x12" PIER.
25' 0"
15' 4"
23' 0"
7' 0"
6' 8"

scale) as 16 is contained in 144 inches, draw F and F' together and parallel with this line from all other points and the result will be equal spacing of 16" for the beams.

Chart XII. Fig. 96. Scale ¼"=1 Ft.

A Framing Plan for a floor laid off by the same system of division of lines.

The length of space to be filled with beams is calculated and reduced to inches then divided by 16" (or the fixed "distance on centres" that the beams are to be placed). If they are to be 12" on centres, it becomes a simple matter of scaling the measurements in the ordinary way, direct without resorting to any formula. 16" on centres is the common practice for constructive reasons.

Do not approximate and **proportion** the spacing as is done in laying off the risers to stairs, but ascertain the greatest number of spacings at the exact distance required (say 16") that is possible, lay them off and leave the final space, to odd measurement as it may come, to be worked out by the mechanic when applying his material in the actual building operation.

Short spacings, those between **"trimmer beams"** or double beams, are equalized to 12" or 16" as nearly as possible from the centre of timbers to which lath may be securely nailed. The common laths for plastering are 4' 0" long and the spacing of 12" or 16" is such as to cover the full length of lath without cutting and at same time making the joinings on the centre of beams for the purpose of the better nailing.

The Key to the situation of beam spacing or the spacing of other timbers to which lath are to be secured, is to provide full nailing and equal bearing of the ends of lath on a beam at same time avoiding the cutting of lath so far as possible.

This applies equally to all ceilings, and side walls whether exterior walls or inner partitions. Wherever common lath of woods are to be applied; when metal lath is used, or "plaster board," as substitute for the regulation wood lath, the spacing of members to which such is to be nailed must be regulated by the exact width or length of the particular material used.

XI.

ELLIPTICAL FORMS.

(Ovals.)

Chart XIII. Fig. 97. Not drawn to scale.

Gives types of elliptical forms. A few of the simple and perhaps best for present needs.

Problem 1: Formed by two circles. The intersection of the circles producing the four necessary centre points from which arcs are swept. The dotted lines drawn through and connecting centre points are extended or prolonged, determines the point of tangency for both connecting arcs. Neither arc should be drawn beyond these dotted lines. **"Axial lines."**

Problem 2: Is a similar method but differing in that the construction is based on **three** circles. The intersection of circles, two in each direction, and through which axial lines are drawn continuously until they converge at a point in one direction and then in the opposite direction far enough to cut the line of ellipse or oval. The centre points of the end circles are the centre points for the lesser arcs; while the point of convergence of the axial lines are the centre points for the greater arcs.

As in the previous example, so is it with all examples; that is, the arcs of circles should stop at the axial lines which at all times is the point of tangency for both connecting arcs.

Problem 3: One-half the minor axis (the perpendicular centre line) is divided into four equal parts, and the same measurement of the four parts revolved to the major axis (the horizontal centre line). Two parts more of same dimension are added outside the revolving arc (dotted line) and the added point from the end is taken as centre point for the lesser arc. The extremities of the minor axis, marked x—x' are taken as centres for the greater arcs.

Problem 4: Draw two parallel lines at any distance. Construct a square on the centre lines, the perpendicular and horizontal axial lines of the oval, the hypotenuse of which square shall be equal to the distance between parallel lines.

Project the lines of square to intersect with parallel lines as radial lines for the arcs of both lesser and greater radii.

The corners of the square, a—b—c—d, indicate the points for all arcs.

Problem 5: A **mechanical** process: To construct an ellipse by intersecting lines: Draw horizontal and perpendicular axial lines. Fix the points of extremity for both length and height of desired oval. From these extremities, draw lines parallel with both horizontal and perpendicular axial lines, and by their intersection producing the corners marked 5. Divide these new made lines into equal parts each way from the centre, both lines in an equal number of parts.

The 0 and 4 points are connected by lines, and the process is continued with all other points in succession and the points of intersection so produced will, if drawn together by a continuous line result in an elliptical form.

The curved line may be drawn free-hand or with French Curves.

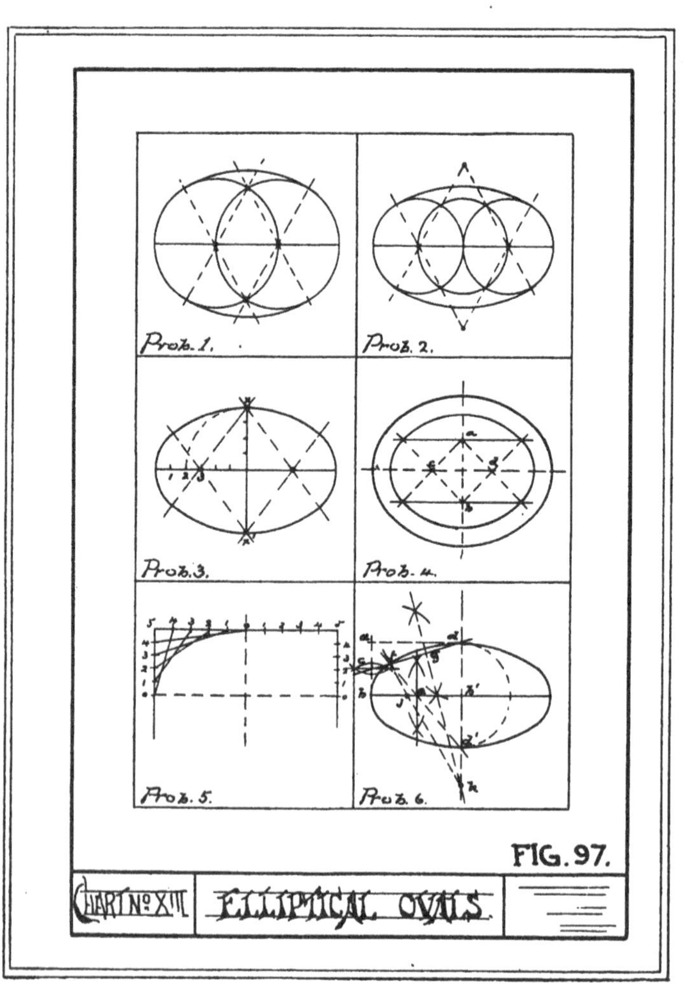
Prob. 1.
Prob. 2.
Prob. 3.
Prob. 4.
Prob. 5.
Prob. 6.
FIG. 97.
CHART Nº XIII
ELLIPTICAL OVALS

Problem 6: The length of major axis and the height of the minor axis being given: Project the extremities, vertically and horizontally to a.

Bi-sect a—b in c.

Draw line from c to d.

Bi-sect line b—b′ in e.

Revolve d to d,′ cutting minor axis.

Draw line from d′ through e cutting line c—d in f.

Bi-sect line f—d in g.

Extend bi-secting line cutting minor axial line in h.

Draw from h to f, cutting major axis in j.

J, is the centre point for the lesser arc.

H, is the centre point for the greater arc.

Application of Ellipse—Chart XIV. Fig 98. Scale 1″=1 Ft.

A simple Colonial Doorway with elliptical head. The trimmings are of stone. The door is of wood with solid panels, no glass, and the Fleur-de-lis represents a "knocker." There is a "Transom" bar over the door and a transom-sash above, which is glazed.

Chart XV. Fig. 99 explains construction and measurements.

Problem 2: Chart XIII. is used in producing the elliptical lines.

Begin with a centre line.

Draw line of bottom of door.

Draw lower line of transom fixing height of door at 7′ 0″.

Draw top line of transom 4″ above, this is also the "springing-line" for arch.

Construct ellipse by drawing the three circles.

Observe carefully the **"radial lines,"** they give direction to the joints between the "**voussoir stones,**" such radial lines for the lesser arcs converge at the near centre point a, while those to the greater arcs radiate from the more distant centre point b.

FIG. 98.

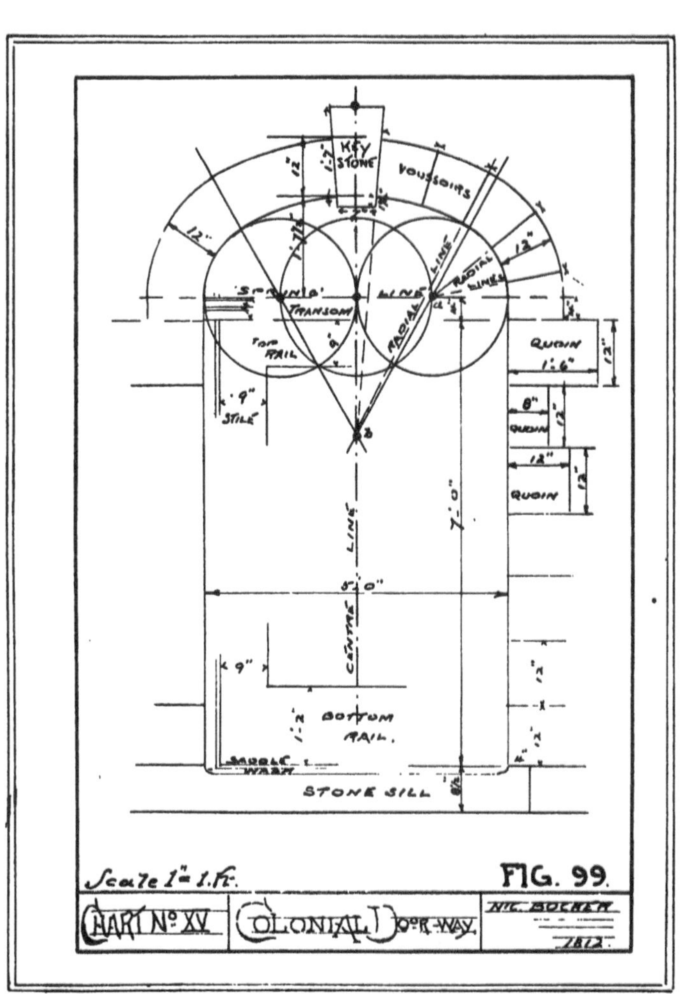
KEY STONE
VOUSSOIRS
12"
SPRINGING LINE
TRANSOM
TOP RAIL
RADIAL LINE
RADIAL LINES
QUOIN
1'6"
9"
STILE
8"
QUOIN
12"
QUOIN
7'0"
CENTRE LINE
5'0"
BOTTOM RAIL.
SADDLE WASH
STONE SILL
Scale 1" = 1 Ft.
FIG. 99.
CHART No. XV
COLONIAL DOOR-WAY
NIC. BOCHER
1912

XII.

THE CENTRE LINE, ITS CONSTRUCTIVE VALUE.

We have learned how to find centres by the use of diagonal lines also something of the value or purpose of such finding. But too much stress cannot be laid upon their usefulness as well as the importance of both centre and diagonal lines. They are indeed invaluable and indispensable to the architectural draftsman. They are infallible guides to location, when correctly used. Also a great convenience from an economic point of view.

Having drawn one-half of an object correctly in measurement and proportion, it becomes a comparatively easy, if not indeed a mere mechanical, process to produce the other half by projection.

A Roof Truss Study—The importance of the center-line system as a guide to correctness may be demonstrated in the laying out of such a thing as a Roof Truss. A careful study of Chart XVI will reveal its importance. Indeed in it lies the foundation for calculating the strength of the truss members either in compression or subject to tensile strain. The use of the centre line insures directness of bearing by relative members and the counteracting of movement.

It also greatly facilitates the work of laying out the various members of a truss. The measurements of all such should be taken from the centre lines as a guide.

In presenting such a problem the Instructor should put the centre line (single line) construction on the black-board with the necessary dimensions marked and such characters as may be necessary to indicate the material to be used, and the student should then be required to produce the finished drawing by the aid of such skeleton outline and markings. Sketch elevations should be given of such parts as may be necessary for intelligent understanding by the pupil.

The centre-line is often an excellent line from which to start a drawing; by its establishment, symmetry is assured and the student should be required to make use of it in all problems where it is available.

There must be a starting line for every drawing and the student is confounded oft-times to know where that line should be and how it should be made. "How shall I start?" or "I do not know how to start," are expressions that often reach the ear of an instructor, and he cannot therefore put too much emphasis on the **starting line,** for each and every problem at the time of its first presentation.

The examples here given will suffice as illustration of actual needs and the way for meeting or serving them.

It may be that the surface of the earth, which in architectural drawing is called the "Ground Line," may be the necessary starting line; or, as in the laying out, or more correctly, laying **up** an elevation of one side of a house, it may be that the top level of the "ground floor," "First Story," or "First Floor" is the better starting line.

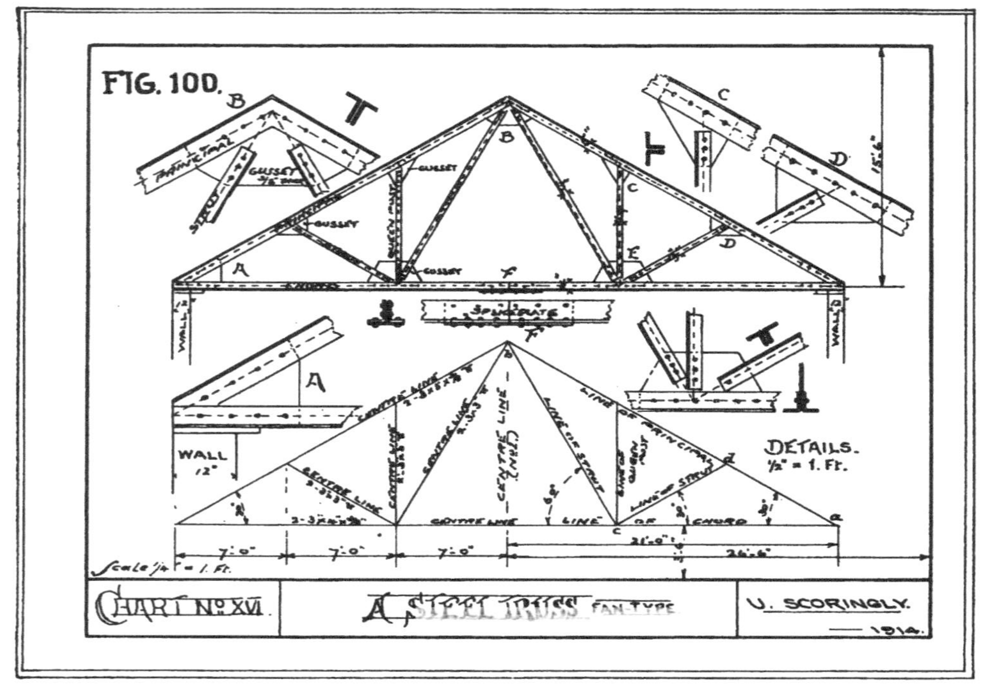
FIG. 100.
GUSSET
DETAILS.
½" = 1. Ft.
WALL
12"
7'·0"
21'·0"
24'·6"
15'·6"
Scale ¼" = 1. Ft.
CHART No. XVI.
A STEEL TRUSS FAN-TYPE
U. SCORINGLY.
1914.

A Simple Form of Roof Truss of Steel.

Chart XVI. Fig. 100. Scale ¼″=1 Ft.

Begin by drawing the skeleton line of truss as shown on the chart, start with centre line of the paper.

Put the lower line of truss, line of chord, in first, 3′—6″ by scale measurement (¼″ to the foot) from the lower margin line.

Fix the length of truss; 21′ 0″ on each side of the centre line. Run lines of Principal rafters at an angle of 30°, use 30° set-square.

Put in the two middle Strut lines at an angle of 60°, starting from the apex of truss marked b (using the 60° set-square for the purpose) and where these lines cut the chord line at c, start the short struts at an angle of 30°.

Erect the perpendicular lines from points of intersection of struts with chord line (or point of convergence of strut lines).

Begin now to draw the lines of the actual Truss above the skeleton as shown on chart. For this new diagram put the centre line of chord 15′ 6″ below upper marginal line.

Put in all centre lines just as drawn in skeleton view below.

Put in all members of truss according to the figures marked on skeleton diagram.

Draw Details last. Being more careful if possible about the exact measurements.

Details should be drawn to the scale of ½″ to the foot.

A Similar Form of Truss Made of Wood.

Chart XVII. Fig 101. Scale ¼″=1 Ft.

Lay out the centre lines as shown in the Steel Truss problem.

Take all guide lines and measurements from Chart

XVIII. Fig. 102. Draw the Truss Elevation, after which draw the Side Elevation, then the Roof Plan, both of which latter figures are to be drawn by orthographic projection, using the T-square and set square in combination. When putting the Purlins on roof plan and side elevation, do not measure their sizes but draw them by projection from the Truss Elevation.

The only measurements to make on the roof plan and side elevation are for the trusses and common rafters, all of which are to be as shown on Fig. 102 as to measurements and position, but the method of drawing them is illustrated by Fig. 84.

Draw the Details last, at a Scale of ½"=1 Ft.

DETAILS
½" = 1 Ft.
C
PRINCIPAL
B
COMMON RAFTER
PURLIN
PRINCIPAL
BLOCK
TRUSS
COMMON RAFTERS
ROOF PLAN
COMMON RAFTER
PURLIN
PRINCIPAL
A
CHORD
WALL
STRUT
KING ROD
SIDE
ELEVATION
TRUSS
ELEVATION.
Scale ½" = 1 Ft.
CHART Nº XVII
A SIMPLE TRUSS of WOOD
S. Mart Jr.
FIG. 101.

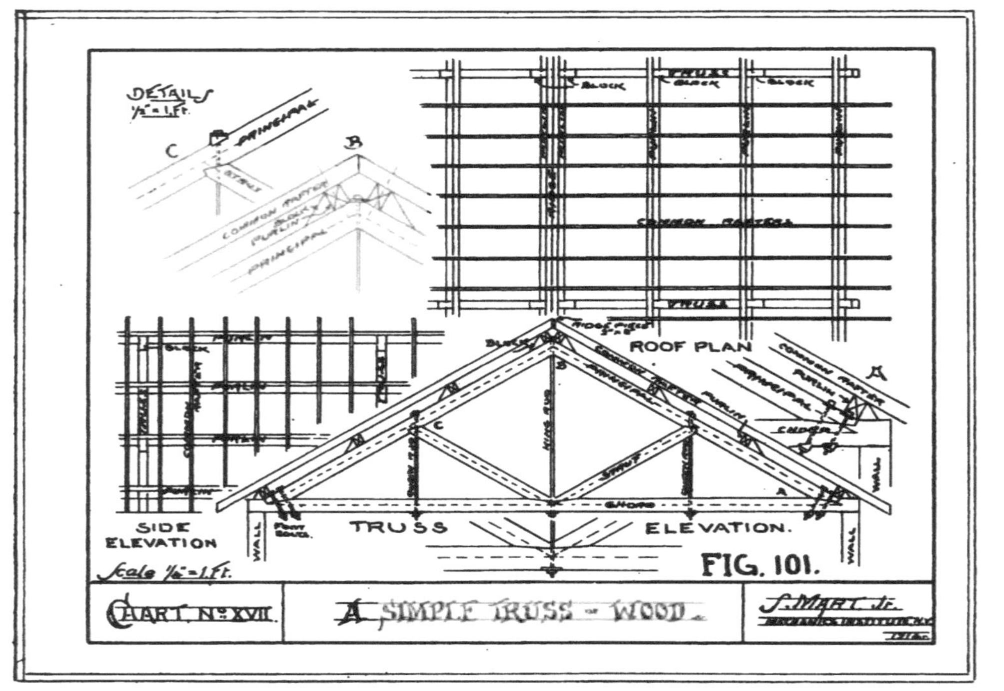

PRINCIPAL
STRUT
PRINCIPAL
PURLIN
TRUSS
RAFTERS
15'-0"
COMMON RAFTERS
2"x6" – 16" ON C.
TRUSS
PRINCIPAL
KING ROD
PURLINS
CHORD
STRUT
CHORD 6"x10"
18'-0"
18'-0"
5'-0"
5'-9"
12"
WALL
STRUT
GIRDER
Scale 1/8" = 1 Ft.
CHART No. XVIII
A LAY-OUT FOR TRUSS OF WOOD
J. MART Jr.
FIG. 102.

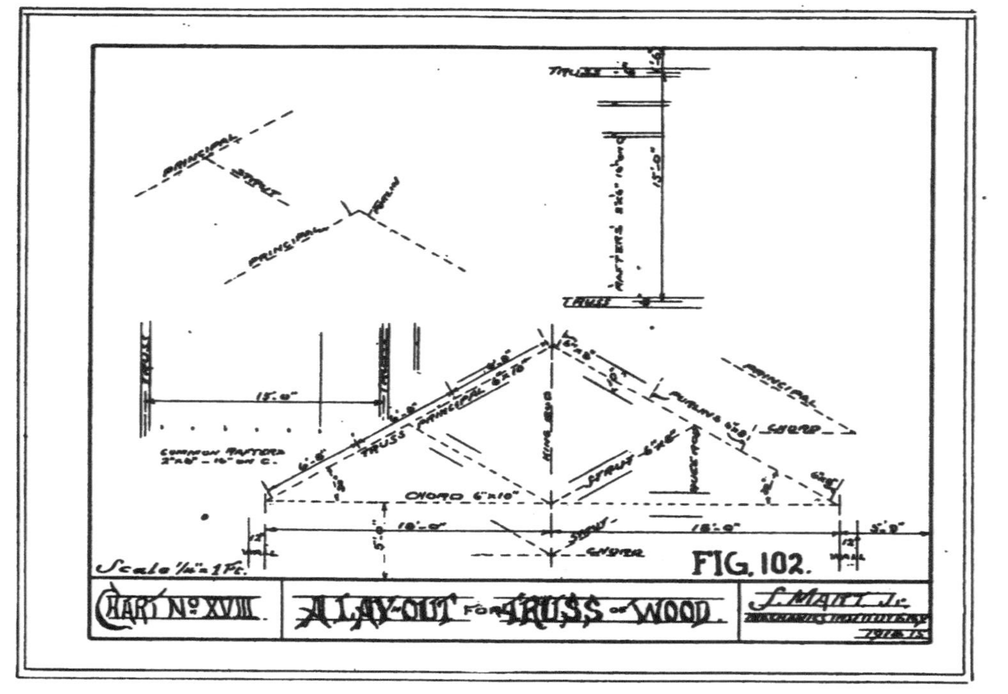

XIII.

A WINDOW FOR A FRAME HOUSE.

Charts XIX-XX-XXI-XXII. Figs. 103-104-105-106.

The specific problem in this instance is to construct the Elevation or rather Elevations, One-half Interior and One-half Exterior of a Window in the wall of a Frame House.

A—A′ represents the elevations required and B and C are the factors from which A-A′ are to be constructed by projection. But as a prerequisite indispensable, we must first learn how to construct B and C. We start with a knowledge of the conventional sizes of the material (see Fig. 105), which we must make use of per-se. The studding* of which the wall of the house is to be framed, has as its greater sectional dimension 4″—i. e., ordinary studding comes in sizes 2″x4″, 3″x4″ and 4″x4″. These are the sizes used for walls and partitions for small houses. Large buildings require thicker walls, necessitating timber of larger "cross section" measurement or "girth."† The thickness of our wall is the first thing to receive attention, and we know that our studding is to be 4″ thick.

There must be a fixed or required size for the window and in the absence of other drawings (plans and elevations) to guide, or other restraint, we will fix the size arbitrarily. Therefore, the window shall be 2′ 0″ wide by 3′4″ high, these are the measurements of the two window sashes combined, and constitute what is technically called the "Day-light opening." Having

*Rough timber for construction of walls and partitions.

†The length of timber does not enter for consideration in problem in hand.

fixed the size of the window we must make mathematical calculation of the space required for the representation of it, and make comparison with the space at command before making a start at the drawing. The first thing to do is to lay out a PLAN of the window, and because of the fixed size of the studding we draw two lines 4" apart marked a, and parallel with bottom marginal line, Fig. 104, Chart No. XX. We are to draw a sectional view also, and an elevation, both in the space above the Plan. We must therefore put the plan in such position that will permit the drawing of that sectional view and that elevation in their proper places and in the space available to make the whole thing appear as symmetrically grouped as may be consistent, and at least, workmanlike. We will, therefore, indicate the width of the sash, 2' 0" by the lines b. We must make provision for the "weight-box" or "boxed frame" for the window. This box frame consists of, first, a "pulley stile" which we will draw 1⅛" thick, next, the "box" or space for sash weights, 2½" will suffice, then the "window stud"; from these figures it will be obvious that a space of 3⅝" will be needed between the line of sash and the studding which forms the rough opening for the window. We will now draw the studding: A so-called "window stud" is usually composed of two pieces of timber 2x4" in cross section—we will draw them. We now have all the necessary perpendicular lines established for one side of the window and the same lines must be repeated on the other side. Then proceed to draw the other parts in the following order: Outside sheathing, outside casing, lath and plaster, sash runners for both upper and lower sashes, parting strips, lower sash lines and inside stop bead, inside grounds, inside architraves, inside stool and outside sill, and with this the **Plan** for window is finished. We must now give attention to the **Sectional View**, for this

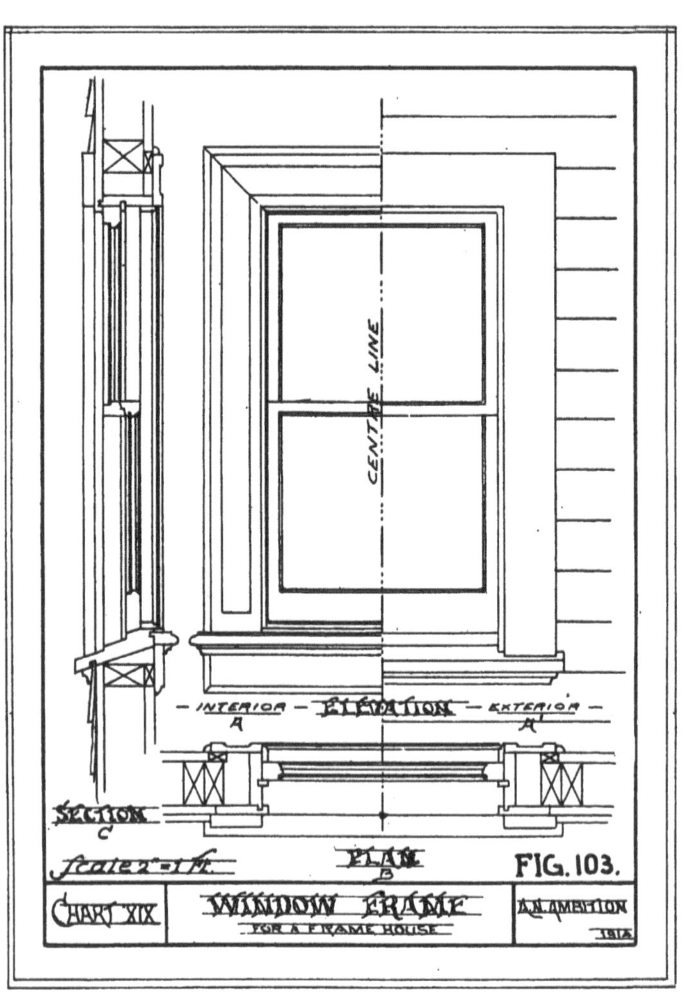
CENTRE LINE
INTERIOR
A
ELEVATION
EXTERIOR
A'
SECTION
C
Scale 2" = 1 Ft.
PLAN
B
FIG. 103.
CHART XIX
WINDOW FRAME
FOR A FRAME HOUSE
A. N. AMBITION
1914

CENTRE LINE
2' 1"
3'-10"
2' 7¼"
2'-0"
6"
4"
Scale 2" = 1 ft.
CHART No. XX
WINDOW LAY-OUT

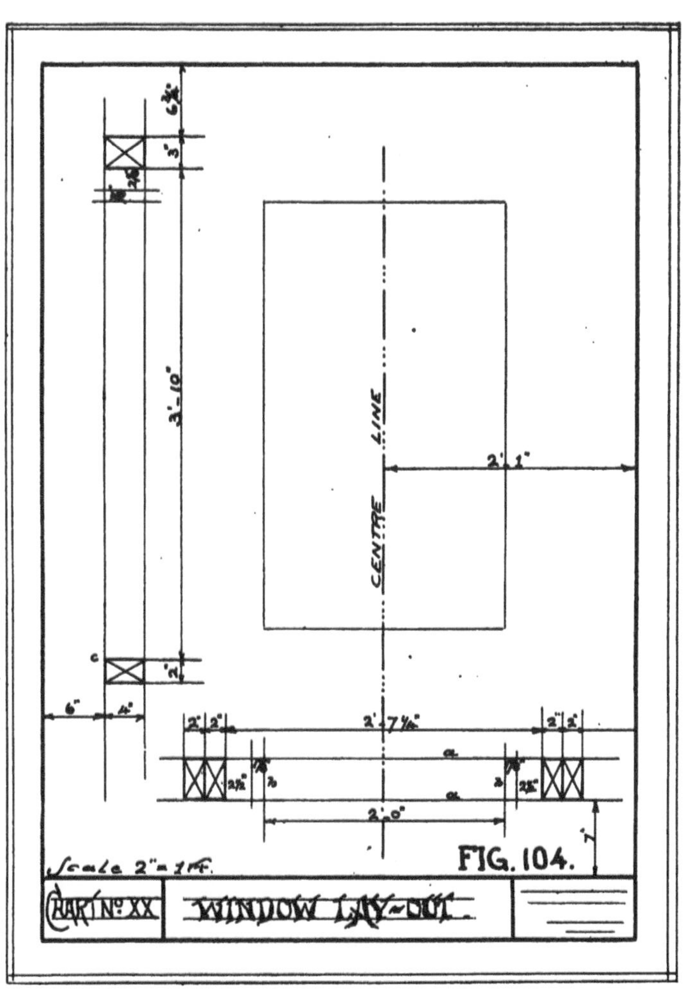

FIG. 104.

there must be a "rough sill" and a "rough head" (door openings have similar heads but not the sill). For present purposes the exact position for the rough sill is an arbitrary matter, except that it should be so placed as to accommodate all that is to follow. We will fix its position therefore as shown in Fig. 104 to the left hand of the sheet and on a line sufficiently above the Plan to permit all necessary detail being drawn in connection with the elevation. The rough sill is a bit of studding, and a 3"x4" will answer the purpose, and as in the plan, the 4" way is thickness of wall. The "finished sill" 2" thick, is now drawn with the under side in contact with the outside "arris" (edge) of rough sill at c. The finished sill must be on an incline, sufficient to turn water off freely, and it must project beyond the finished face of clap-boards, etc., for similar protection, and to insure water (rain storms) remaining outside the building, and prevented following the underside of sill, back into the rough frame work by capillary attraction, a "weathering" or "groove" is "plowed" into the underside of the sill overhang, to receive the topmost edge of a clap-board. This grooving is also known as a "drip" or a "lip." The top of sill is "rebated" or plowed to produce another type of weathering for the prevention of water forcing its way back by wind-pressure, under the bottom rail of sash, and so finding lodgement on the face of plastering beneath the "apron" of inside sill or "stool" to window. All of these minor details are drawn in connection with sill, then the sheathing and clap-boards on the outside of frame. The stool, grounds, and lath and plaster on the inside. The lines of the studding are now projected from the rough sill or stud beneath the sill, in an upward direction to, approximately, the position for the window head, and a "rough head" inserted. This is also a bit of studding, and a 2"x4" will answer. The exact height of this rough head above the rough sill is governed by the height of sash plus the space occupied by the finished sill, and the space which will be needed for the finished head to window.

The "head jamb" will be ⅞" thick and we will provide 2" for clearance space. This last is necessary to safe-guard against damage to window by dint of settlement, caused by deflection of the rough head as a result of pressure from above, also the weight of floor beams and the load contingent thereon. After locating head jamb, it, and the finished sill are connected by a series of perpendicular lines representing upper and lower sashes, sash runners, parting strip, inside and outside stop-beads, architraves and outside casing or "fascias" are added. All of which are taken by actual measurement from corresponding parts as drawn on the plan beneath (see Fig. 105), and revolving them from a horizontal position to the perpendicular, and transforming the arrises* of the members on the plan into lines to represent a face view or elevation of the members corresponding. The head jamb is fitted also with parting strip, stop beads, architrave, outside head casing or fascia, etc. All to correspond with the pulley stile or "hanging stile" section as shown on plan. The sheathing, clap-boards, grounds and lath and plaster are added just as has been done below the sill.

"Top rail," lock rail (meeting rail), and bottom rail of sashes are put in the runners to represent both upper and lower sashes. And with this the sectional view will have been completed.

The half-elevation of the exterior and half-elevation of the interior now alone remain to be drawn, and that is accomplished without making a single measure-

*Arrises are sharp corner edges.

(EXTERIOR)
(INTERIOR)
(PLAN.)
Scale 3" = 1 Ft.
CHART No. XXI
DETAILS
DIMENSIONED PARTS.
FIG. 105.

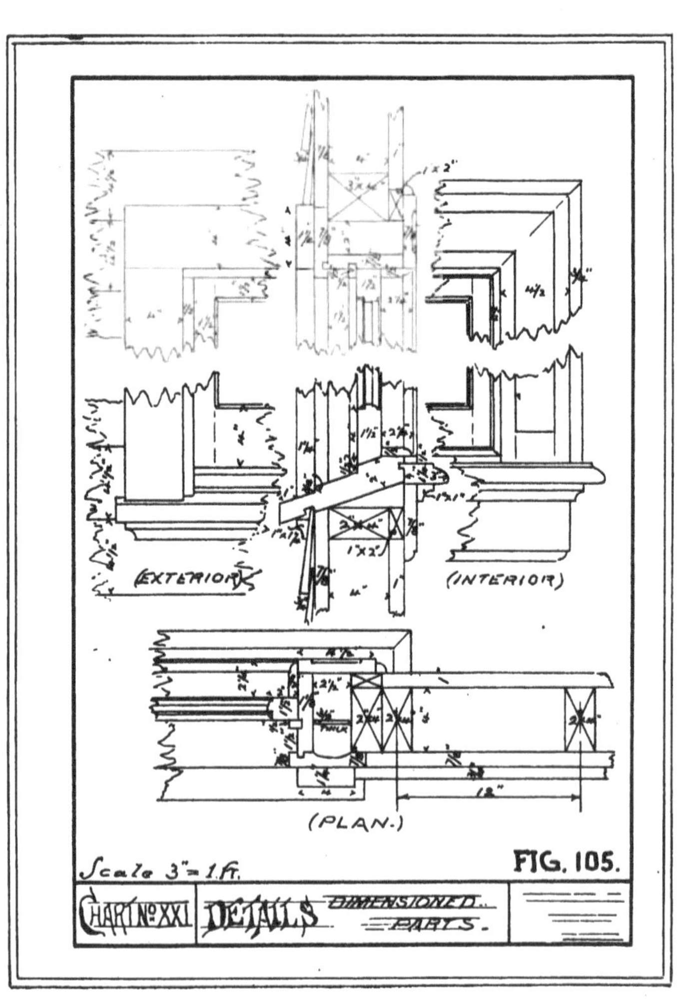

CLAPBOARD
FASCIA
OUTSIDE STOP
TOP RAIL
SASH
(GLASS)
STILE
BOTTOM RAIL
SILL
BED MOULD
(EXTERIOR)
CLAPBOARDS
FLASHING
SHEATHING
LATH & PLASTER
GROUND
ROUGH HEAD
HEAD CASING
HEAD JAMB
ARCHITRAVE
BLIND STOP
OUTSIDE STOP
SASH RUNNER
INSIDE STOP BEAD
GLASS
STILE
STOOL
COVE
APRON
ROUGH SILL
GROUND STRIP
SHEATHING
(INTERIOR)
STOOL
ARCHITRAVE
BACK BAND
GROUND
LATH & PLASTER
INSIDE STOP BEAD
WINDOW STUDS
STUD
SASH RUNNER
SHEATHING
CLAPBOARD
BLIND STOP
OUTSIDE CASING
OUTSIDE CASING
(PLAN.)
Scale 3" = 1 Ft.
CHART No. XXII
DETAILS PARTS NAMED

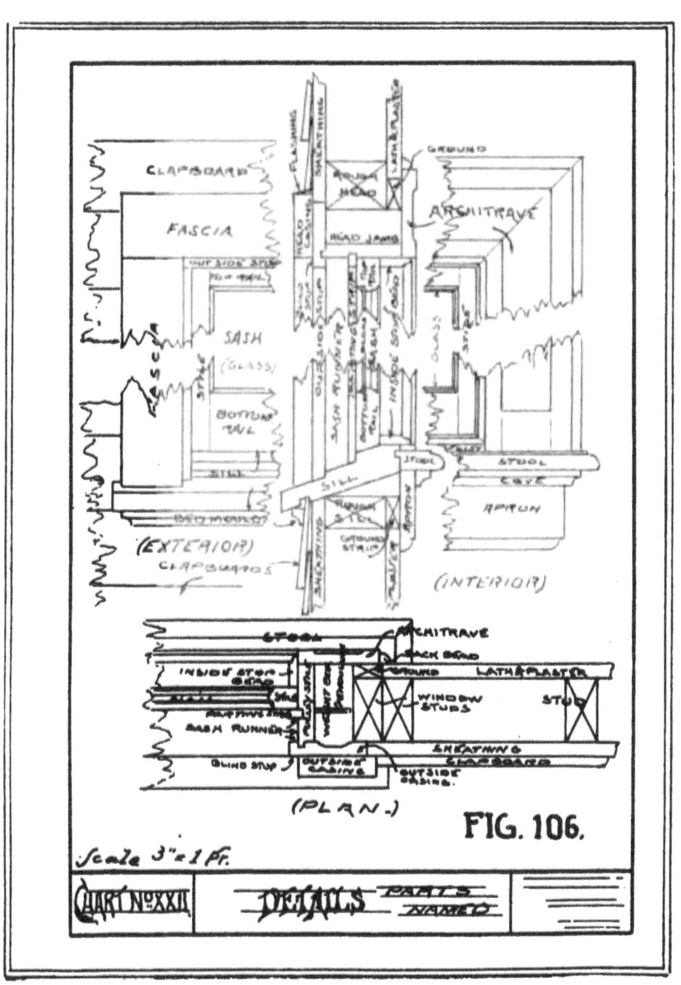

FIG. 106.

ment, in fact, the process is reduced to a mere mechanical one, since it is a matter of the simple straight projection of lines,—perpendicularly from the plan, and horizontally from the sectional view. The intersection of these two systems of lines makes the projection of the elevations possible from the two other views. All members should now be marked with their respective terms (see Fig. 106) (it is customary to do so). The general titles added, and the chart is completed.

The preceding problem is mainly a matter of orthographic projection, and the arrangement of the different views, their relation to each other, and the method of producing them is typical of what should be done in all similar problems. In short, the three views shown by such a drawing—Plan, Section and Elevation are necessary to explain each and every measurement and the detail parts in the three dimensions of space, that is, height, breadth and depth.

This problem should not be given students as an entirety; but they should be required to make the plan, also the sill in the sectional view, from rough sketches, perhaps free-hand on the black-board, and without scale, as a suggestive guide. Or by a chart on enlarged scale.

In either case the dimensions should be marked on the various members (see Fig. 105) that the student may work from them. (The student cannot be expected to know these things without prompting.)

The student should be required to produce the head to the window by projecting lines from the sill up for the verticals and taking measurements from the plan for the horizontal lines. And after the plan and sectional drawing is finished he should construct the elevations, interior and exterior, by projection from both plan and section, for vertical and horizontal lines according to the relative positions of the several parts.

XIV.

OUTER WALL FOR A FRAME HOUSE.

Chart XXIII. Fig. 107. Scale 2″=1 Ft., represents a problem which is embraced by the course for beginners at the Cooper Union, New York City. It is part of an outer wall for a frame house. This problem, also the one which will follow next in order, has been analyzed and arranged by the author to conform to the system herein advocated. A commendable feature of the method of instruction in vogue at Cooper Union is the use of color to represent materials, rather than the more mechanical system of hatching with lines. The use of color is the method most in favor with practicing architects, the world over; its use adds materially to the appearance of a drawing, and facilitates the reading of it, which is an advantage not to be minimized or in any way regarded as least. The use of color gives zest to the novitiate and inspires the student to greater effort.

The particular features of the problem in hand are: A simple form of **watertable,** at the connection between the frame work of superstructure with the foundation wall on which it rests. And a **boxed-cornice,** Colonial type, with a gutter of metal applied in a way not to obscure or deface the **crown-mould** of cornice.

Chart XXIV, Fig. 108, gives analysis and directs in the laying out, and proceeding with the entire drawing systematically to a finish.

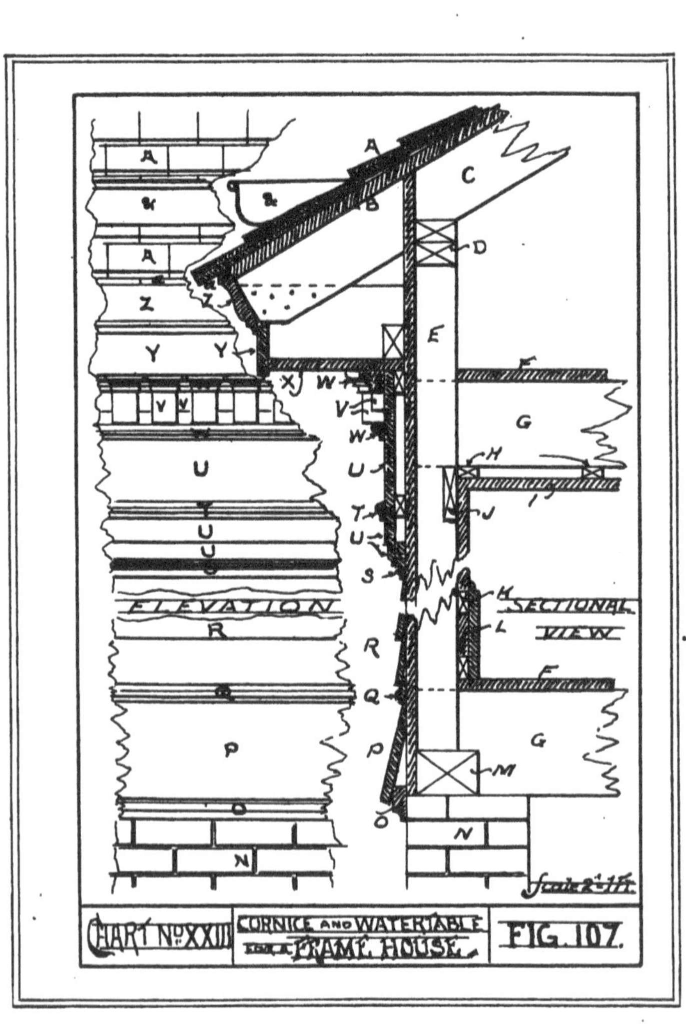

CHART No. XXIII — CORNICE AND WATERTABLE FOR A FRAME HOUSE — FIG. 107.

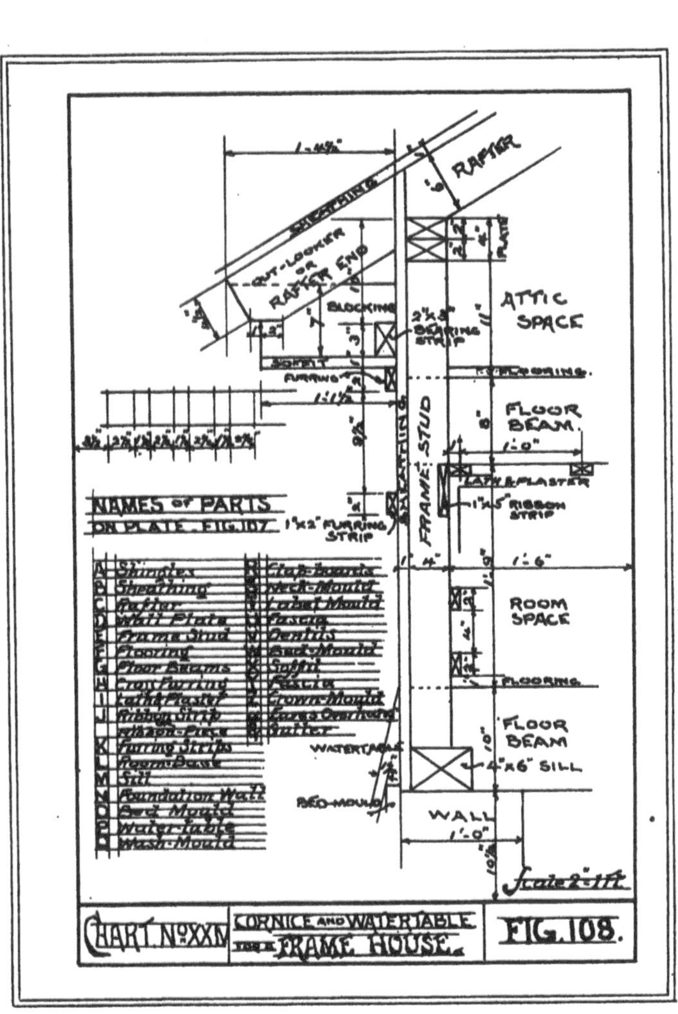

RAFTER
SHEATHING
OUT-LOOKER OR RAFTER END
BLOCKING
BEARING STRIP
SOFFIT
FURRING
ATTIC SPACE
FLOORING
FLOOR BEAM
SHEATHING
FRAME STUD
LATH & PLASTER
RIBBON STRIP
FURRING STRIP
NAMES OF PARTS ON PLATE FIG. 107
ROOM SPACE
FLOORING
FLOOR BEAM
WATERTABLE
4"x6" SILL
BED-MOULD
WALL
Scale 2"-1 Ft.
CHART No XXIV
CORNICE AND WATERTABLE FOR A FRAME HOUSE
FIG. 108.

The names of parts as given will materially assist in intelligent understanding of the assembled members and their relation to each other.

Begin by drawing two vertical lines, one of them 1′-6″ from the marginal line at the right as representing the inside line of **studding**; make a second line, 4″ to the left of the first, as representing the thickness of stud.

Draw these two lines very nearly the full length of space between top and bottom marginal lines. It is of course assumed that the marginal lines and trimming lines have been established and drawn on all sheets previously prepared.

Draw a horizontal line to represent the top of foundation wall, 10½″ above top marginal line to the **title panel.** Lay off all measurements on a vertical line as shown to locate floor beams, and **wall plate.** Draw lines representing these members. From this on, follow the order given below for all detail work.

Draw the lines of roof rafters at an angle of 30° starting at the topmost, inner arris of plate. Rafter to be 6″ high. Roof sheathing next, 1″ thick. Wall sheathing, 1″ thick. Ribbon strip, 1″x5″. All furring strips, including **cross furring** to ceiling, 1″x2″-12″ on centres (that is, 12″ from the centre of one strip to the centre of another strip). Base furring strips (**grounds**). Cornice furrings, Bearing strip, 2″x3″, Blocking, 7″ high, Soffit, Fascia, Crown-mould, Fascia, Dentils, Bed-moulds, Label-mould and Neck-mould.

Water-table, Wash-mould, Clap-boards, lath and Plaster, and room Base. Brick lines in foundation wall, all shingles on roof and metal gutter. All of which when done completes the **Sectional View.** The remainder of the drawing is an **Elevation** of all face work. All lines for the elevation should be made with a T-square by projection, direct from the sectional view.

The only measurements to be made in this connection are, the width of shingles, 6″, and the dentils and the spacing of them.

The drawing is now made and ready for marking with names of parts, and putting on of dimensions. But, before doing this, we will introduce a technique of draftsmanship as yet not made use of in this book.

Shade-Lining*—An embellishment and finish, not always resorted to or applied to an architectural drawing, though when so used, it is always an advantage. It gives relief to relative parts, divides and segregates solids from space and gives much **vim** and **snap** to a drawing. Shade-lining is accomplished by setting the drawing pen to a gauge, coarser than that used for the work in general, and producing a heavier, consequently blacker line. It will be observed that such lines are drawn on the right side, and also on the lower side or edge of all solids; and where a solid overlaps a solid, that fact is made apparent by the use of shade lines. For example: The out-looker or rafter-end overlaps the blocking to which it is nailed. The stud overlaps the beams which pass behind studs as shown by dotted lines (nailing is not shown here because the nails are driven from the opposite side, through the beams into the studding). The student should make a careful study of the shade-lines on the elevation, which will reveal the fact that all over-hanging **arises,** which would in nature cast a shadow, are regarded as **shade lines.**

The student should pay particular heed to the way shade lines are used on brick work in elevation. The brick work in sectional view should not be shade lined.

Chart XXV. Figure 109. Scale 1″=1 Ft., Details: Scale 2″=1 Ft.

*This book does not deal with *shade* and *shadow*.

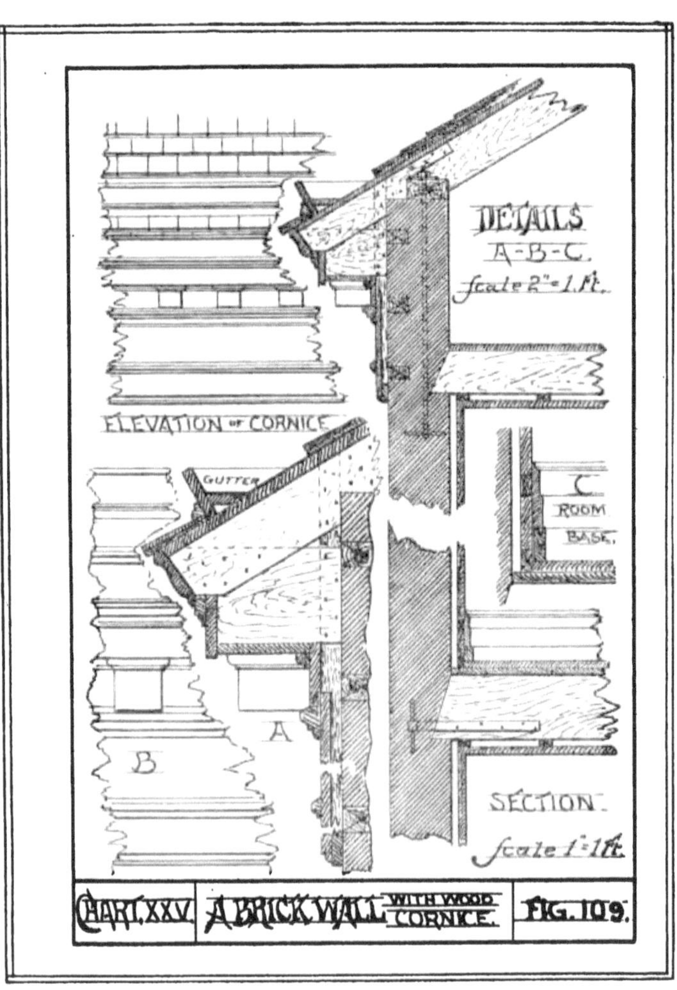
DETAILS
A-B-C
Scale 2" = 1 Ft.
ELEVATION OF CORNICE
GUTTER
C
ROOM
BASE
A
B
SECTION
Scale 1" = 1 Ft.
CHART. XXV.
A BRICK WALL WITH WOOD CORNICE.
FIG. 109.

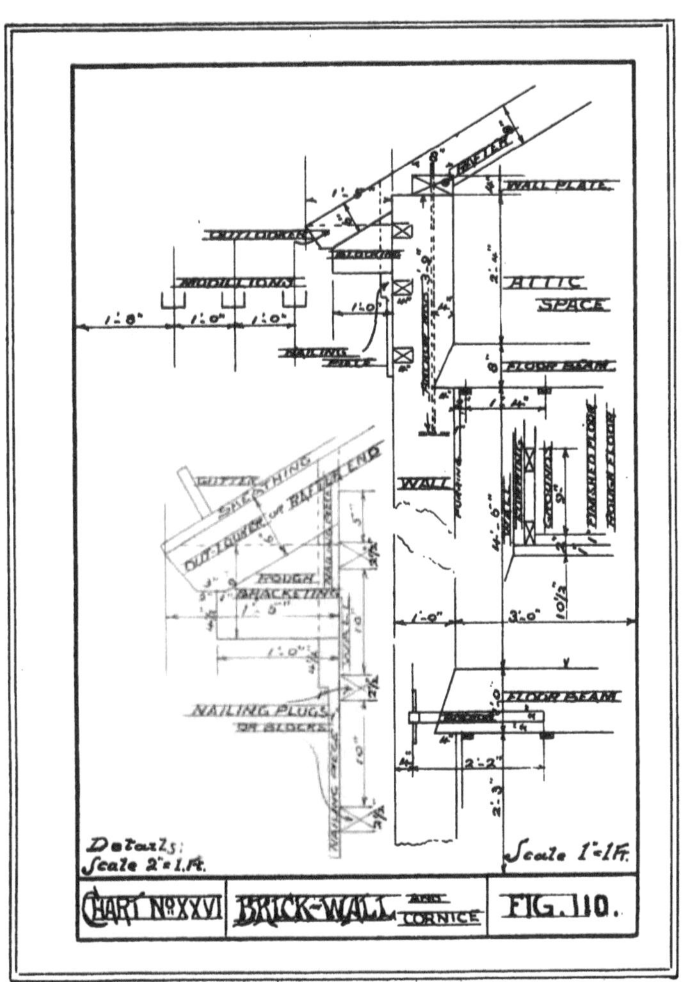

RAFTER
WALL PLATE
OUT-LOOKER
BLOCKING
MODILLIONS
ATTIC
SPACE
NAILING PIECE
FLOOR BEAM
WALL
FURRING
GROUNDS
FINISHED FLOOR
ROUGH FLOOR
GUTTER
SHEATHING
OUT-LOOKER or RAFTER END
ROUGH BRACKETING
NAILING PLUGS OR BLOCKS
FLOOR BEAM
Details; Scale 2" = 1 Ft.
Scale 1" = 1 Ft.
CHART No. XXVI
BRICK-WALL AND CORNICE
FIG. 110.

This is another chart based on the regular course at Cooper Union. It represents an outer wall of a brick house with cornice, roof construction in connection with wall, and room base (a part of interior trim). The cornice and base are shown, more clearly, at the enlarged scale of 2"=1 Ft. Chart XXVI, Fig. 110, explains the method of producing the entire drawing. Start from the marginal line at the right; draw a vertical line, 3' 0" from it, and 1' 0" from this draw a second vertical line. Fix height of floor beams and wall plate, just as was done in the preceding study (Frame House Wall). Draw the wall plate and anchor —roof rafter—nailing blocks or plugs ("wooden bricks"), furring of brick wall (on the inside), cross-furring to both ceilings (on the underside of floor beams), beam anchor, cornice blocking. All other items of detail are to follow in the same manner as described in the previous example.

After all parts are drawn, do the **cross-hatching** as shown: Observe carefully that the direction of the lines of hatching is such not to interfere with lines of joints, or the contour lines of mouldings or other forms. Also observe that each separate piece of wood is clearly in evidence as retaining its individuality; this is accomplished by reversing the direction of the lines in hatching. Observe further, that the **nailing piece** which is secured to plugs in brick wall for the purpose of carrying cornice members is hatched with short **vertical** lines, which, together with dotted lines and nailings, shows very clearly that this nailing-strip extends full depth of cornice,* and across the rafter end, stopping at the roof sheathing. Thus firmly securing all parts, **en masse.**

*The cornice complete is called an "*Entablature.*"

All solid sticks of **timber*** are hatched with **curved** lines as representing end grain as shown by growth-rings. The elevation or side view of wood surfaces, beams, rafter, rough bracketing, etc., are done with lines much elongated to represent "combing" or face view of grain. Cross cut sections of all wood and brick work are hatched in this drawing. Face surfaces of **rough** "lumber" only are "grained."

Surfaces of finished work are not hatched, grained or "rendered"† in any way other than **shade-lined.**

*"*Timber*" means squared dimensioned lumber. "*Lumber*" includes dimensioned timber, boards, plank, scantlings, etc. In short, it comprises *all wood.*

†"*Rendered*" means "worked-up or finished to a degree more or less pictorial.

XV.

ARCHITECTURAL LETTERING.

It is important the architectural draftsman should be able to letter fairly well, and in many cases he should be able to do so even well. It is not necessary, neither is it desirable that lettering should be done in the stiff, mechanical and painfully exact way so prevalent with engineers and surveyors, for whom there is perhaps a justification in very large measure.

The average survey of property is a simple, single line diagram, and minus the painfully wrought lettering of Title and descriptive notes would make a slim showing as a work of art. Lettering therefore becomes a necessity with him as a matter of detail as well as embellishment, if such a draftsman would have his drawings appear to best advantage.

The subjects of the drawing, by architectural draftsmen as a rule, are in themselves sufficiently interesting and attractive perhaps, to please the eye of the beholder without the aid of embellishment by lettering. Nevertheless, lettering is with the architectural draftsman an essential. Titles and submarkings must be constantly employed as part of a language peculiarly belonging to architectural art. A Graphic Dictionary as it were, to insure understanding of graphic forms which might otherwise be misread by the novice as being hieroglyphic. Lettering then, becomes an interpreter of form and should therefore be simple, legible and sufficiently true to conventional forms or ideas of what letters should be, that they may be intelligently understood.

The author has neither sympathy with nor use for **nondescript** letters. There can be no justification for a U appearing in V form under the guise of being **artistic.** Such things are mere fads, eccentric foibles, and illy applied flourishes; an unwarranted adaptation of an obsolete form by art enthusiasts who are apparently incapable of adjudging between the **oddly curious** and the truly artistic. To them anything odd is the correct thing to do if one would be classed among the "upper ten" of his profession; "the more's the pity" because it frequently occurs that design of real merit is marred by such blemish.

The above arraignment should suffice to convince any draftsman of intelligence of the absurdity of such fads and thereby guide him to a consistent handling of this phase of architectural draftsmanship.

The student should fix upon a style of lettering most suitable to his own hand and most consistent with the class of work he is employed in doing. He should cultivate that style and become proficient in it; (better to have familiarity with one style, and be able to do it well, than a mere smattering of many styles).

A knowledge of many styles of lettering is the province of the sign painter or "sign writer," the lithographer, the engraver and the engrosser.

The architectural student will have but small occasion to use the stiff mechanical letters, but when prompted to employ them he should confine himself to the plain forms; of which that style known to the printer as "Gothic" (see Fig. 113), is perhaps best.

Block letters are also consistent and desirable, they may be solid or in outline; shaded or unshaded, more often they are unshaded. "The Old-Style," Colonial* (so-called) are eminently suitable and befitting archi-

*All so-called "*Colonial*" design classifies as adaptation of classic art.

ARCHITECTURAL rrrr

LETTERING

ARCHITECTURAL

PRACTICE FREE HAND

FREEDOM of HAND

ABCDEFGHIJK.

ABCDEFGHIJKLMNOPQ.

small letters;-abcdefgh.

VARIETY

not necessary but a

SIMPLE STYLE is

BEST

FIG. 111.

tectural drawings. They are artistic (if shorn of fad nondescript forms, i. e., by using a U for a U and a V for a V, an S for an S and an F for an F. Without permitting either to encroach on the prerogatives of the other) whether such letters are made with instruments or free-hand and in outline or solid black they are equally commendable. Deviation from true conventional types or forms are permissible provided a true form is not so distorted and maltreated as to become illegible or at least confusing to the understanding.

As a rule the Roman style of letters should be avoided, it has its use, however, in architectural work, but there are forms much more desirable for use in common practice. For our purpose nothing can be more consistent or appropriate than a simple form of free-hand lettering, ever ready, quickly done and consistent.

The natural, reasonable crudeness, if you please, of hand work, gives artistic value to such character of lettering.† Crudeness does not, neither should it, typify carelessness or slovenness.

Free-hand lettering should be done with reasonable neatness, not painfully, but carefully done. The draftsman has no calling in competition with a type cutter (of old, or "matrix" maker to-day), for printers' use.

The **Spacing** of letters is a matter of some scientific as well as artistic consequence to the sign writer and professional letterer, but the artist drafstman has but little occasion to worry about that detail, since for his special needs, his practiced eye for proportion and the general fitness of things, should prompt him to

†Just in same ratio that the marks of the hammer gives to wrought iron, and sheet metal work, and the chisel marks imparts to a carving. Hand-work should stand for its own, and not compete with machine stamped goods.

automatically space letters just as is the case in his chirographic lettering (ordinary writing with a pen).

The above is enough for the purpose of this textbook, in extenuation of theory; so now, a few words on the more practical phase of the subject are in order.

The theoretical dissertation above touches on the practical as to fitness and the general character of lettering that should and should not be used for architectural purposes, and a few simple suggestions should make the practical side of the subject easy for the beginner.

Simple line forms of letters are best for the novice to practice at the beginning, avoid all embellishments and flourishes. Do not attempt to put letters in ink until they have first been made in lead pencil. Regulate the general height of letters, and at same time preserve alignment by the use of horizontal guide lines, top and bottom, in lead pencil. Such lines may be put in ink at the finish with good result and it sometimes enhances the sketchiness of the work and gives a certain value not apparent if omitted. Such lines assist in improving the appearance of the alignment making it more uniform and seem truer even when irregularities do exist in the actual height of the letters.

If a perpendicular style is employed—all perpendicular lines should be reasonably perpendicular—an important essential in lettering is that all letters should be consistent as to direction.* One inclining in one direction and another in another, gives a "crazy-quilt" distortion and consequent discontent to the beholder. If letters are sloping either forward or backward they should be uniformly so. As a rule an inclined letter is more easily made; and irregularities in the finished work less noticeable. Such forms of

*There are exceptions in types of Colonial and irregular types.

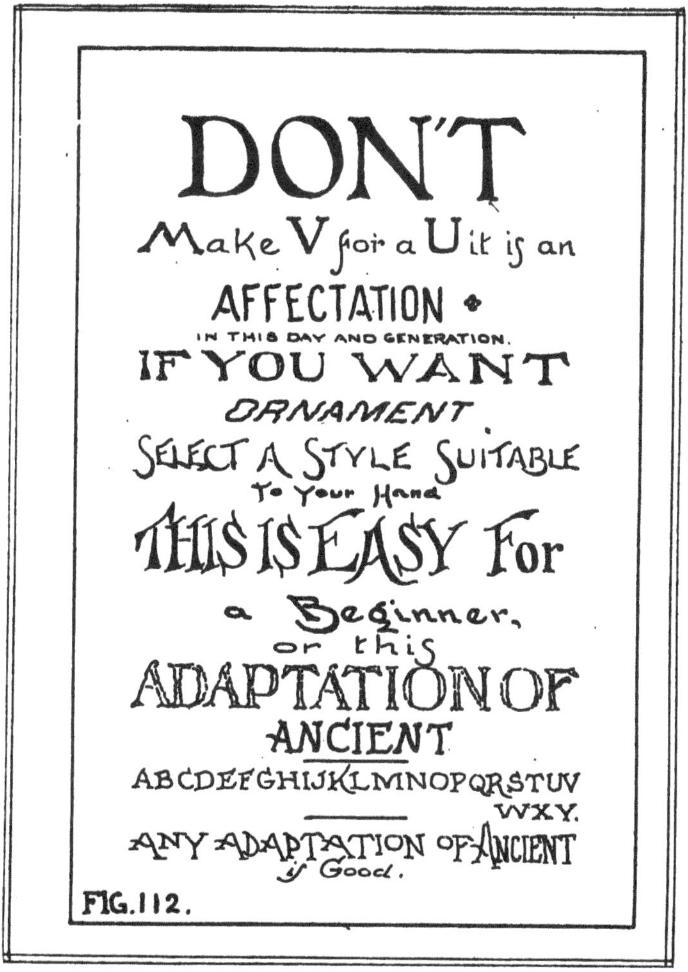

DONT

Make V for a U it is an

AFFECTATION

IN THIS DAY AND GENERATION.

IF YOU WANT

ORNAMENT

SELECT A STYLE SUITABLE

To Your Hand

THIS IS EASY For

a Beginner,

or this

ADAPTATION OF

ANCIENT

ABCDEFGHIJKLMNOPQRSTUV

WXY.

ANY ADAPTATION OF ANCIENT

if Good.

FIG. 112.

letters wherein straight lines are avoided, are of all perhaps, the most easily made to appear free from distortion or imperfections. They are classified as of the **Rustic** type, and may partake of the characteristics or style of any of the standard examples or styles. The unadorned "Gothic," or the more free but equally refined "Colonial." They may depart from conventional ideas; and originality and even uniqueness in characteristics may obtain. ("Unique" does not mean oddly-curious nondescripts.) A design of letters may be unique with a high degree of merit just as design in any other department is possible. It is much easier to make a rustic letter than one more staid, and to do so, a freedom in handling the pen or pencil must be cultivated; avoid a cramped restrained condition of the fingers and hand, practice free action; do not worry over first crudeness, practice will adjust matters and result in automatically preserving balance or equipoise. As before advised, do all lettering first in lead pencil before attempting to put them in ink, unless you become expert.

It will pay for the effort, if a little time is devoted to the centering of a **Title** with the subject, or at least properly placing a title. It is not necessary neither is it customary to put a title under the subject and on centre, it may be at one side, or any where on the paper where it may serve to best advantage, but in all cases there should be a reason for it and it should be symmetrically done. Again: The use of the lead pencil first will save vexation and possible disappointment.

It is at all times in better taste* and a much more refined practice, to use one style or character of letter only on a drawing: except in some instances, capitalization may be made with a form of letter harmoni-

*Taste is a matter of intellectual culture, not merely a matter of individual opinion.

ously differing from the "text," or "matter" in general.

Ecclesiastic styles of letters are eminently appropriate for the marking of drawings of ecclesiastic subjects, fragmentary or assembled composition.

The subject of lettering is an art by itself, one to which a special volume might with perfect consistency be devoted, and one which should not trespass more on the limitations of this text-book. It must suffice therefore to say, there is such a thing as consistency and appropriateness of style of lettering to the subject labeled which is to be learned by experience only.

THIS IS GOTHIC SO-CALLED, &
THIS IS
BLOCK STYLE-
ARCHITECTURAL
DRAWING AND READING

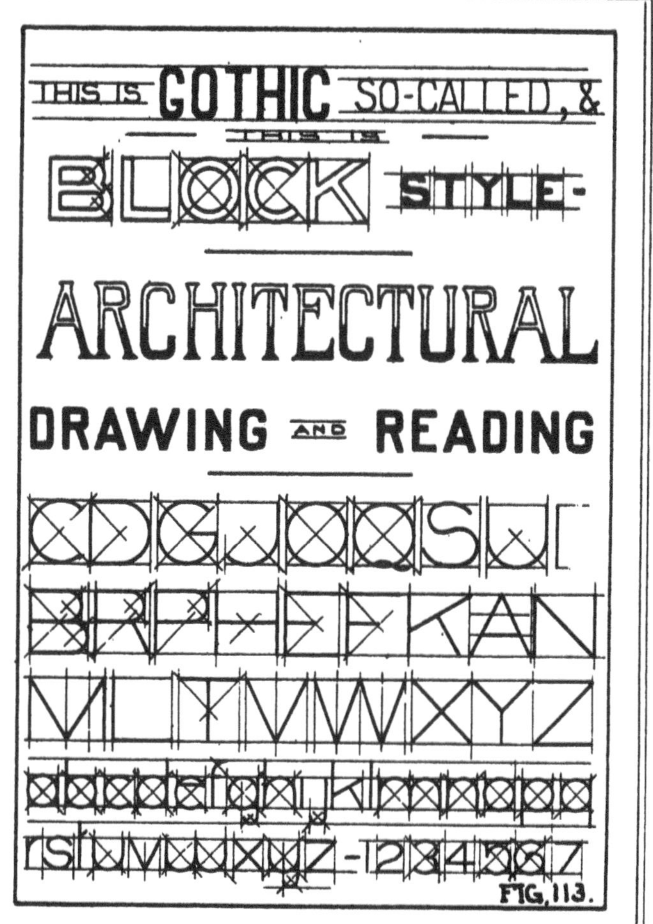

FIG. 113.

XVI.

CONVENTIONS IN ARCHITECTURAL DRAWINGS.

One can hardly hope to escape so-called "**conventions**" of form, and practice, in connection with a productive pursuit.

Neither are there any rules so "hard and fast" as to enslave the architectural draftsman. He remains a "free-lance" notwithstanding the existence of **conventions**—more particularly those which have crept in his profession of recent years to supercede perhaps, those time honored customs and practices which have prior right to recognition. Reference is made to the introduction of certain systems of lines, etc., as substitute for color to represent material. These new forms of conventions have their place but are not so important to the architectural draftsman, generally speaking, as would seem to be a reality according to the authors of most books of recent years publication on architectural drawing.

The specific use of lines to represent color, seem to lay in the facility with which such things may be reproduced by blue-printing or similar reproduction processes.

That such formula or system may be of value to the engineer or to the **technical** draftsman, in general—goes without question, but for the purposes of architectural drawing it is difficult to find a fitting substitute for color. In architectural drawing the surfaces and members or various parts to be covered are so numerous and so extensive as to render any "hatching"* process laborious. Besides: there are no systems which may be consistently regarded as **standard.** Standard for all.

The U. S. Naval Department has its standard. The Mechanical Draftsmen have theirs. The Electrical Engineer, Surveyors and Patent Office draftsman,, Landscape Architect, and others have codes peculiar to their special needs, but these do not seem to standardize and the difference in representation of certain material are at least at times confusing. So much so, that it is a common practice where the hatching processes are employed; to supplement each drawing so rendered, with a "Key Chart," explanatory of the **conventions** used on that particular drawing. Indeed, in the present condition of things, this is the only safe way of insuring correct reading of architectural plans when so conventionalized, and at best, even under these conditions there is more or less confusion. The multiplicity of lines used in hatching and their variation renders many drawings a "maze" of line which confuse and confound the reading of measurements (figures) and other necessary explanatory markings. The array of lines, alternately black and white, is often dazzling and they are equally so, in white and blue.

The time honored custom of using color, Red, to represent brickwork, Yellow, for all wood-work, Gray, or Blue, or Brown, for stone, Blue, for iron, Green, for glass, etc., and the density of color regulated by the density of material represented (either in cross section or surface) is much to be preferred and recommended for ordinary or general practice. The colors approximating the natural color of the various material so closely, that the reading of material is

*Hatching, means filling-in or finishing with short lines or similar rendering to represent cross-cut sections.

done at a glance, and that without any confusion with other detail markings.

Water Colors are best to use on drawing paper, also on tracing cloth* (Vellum), but crayon pencils (so-called colored lead pencils) are much better for use on blue-prints; they are more quickly applied, therefore more practical. Tracings on either Vellum or paper should not be colored, if most satisfactory blue-prints are expected from them. For large scale drawings and full size sections, colored pencils or larger colored crayons are best.

There are many conventional forms and methods for indicating certain fixtures and features or units in plan making, but they are too numerous for extended consideration in a book for beginners.

There are, however, two or three **"conventions"** which should be pointed out to the beginner as things to be avoided.

If he is making drawings for exhibition purposes only; there is of necessity, and justly so, much more latitude and freedom to be exercised in the method of representing things, also in the "rendering," but when the drawings are intended for **practical use** by practical men, the superfluities should be avoided.

For the practical man the drawings should be simple, plain and clear. It is very bad practice, though indulged in by many capable draftsmen, to pass a corner or the intersection of lines by extending the lines in either direction beyond the point of contact.† Fig. 114 shows the way it is often done, while Fig. 115 presents the same subject with corners and intersections as they should be made.

*A linen fabric specially prepared as a medium on which to copy drawing by tracing.

†It is legitimate and even desirable, as a convenience, to permit lines to pass when laying out an original rough draft, for the purpose of indicating the point of intersection wi'h more or less emphasis, but such crudity should never be permitted to remain on a finished drawing.

If an elevation or sectional drawing should be made with such extended lines it would be worthless because of the confusion of lines, and the disfigurement

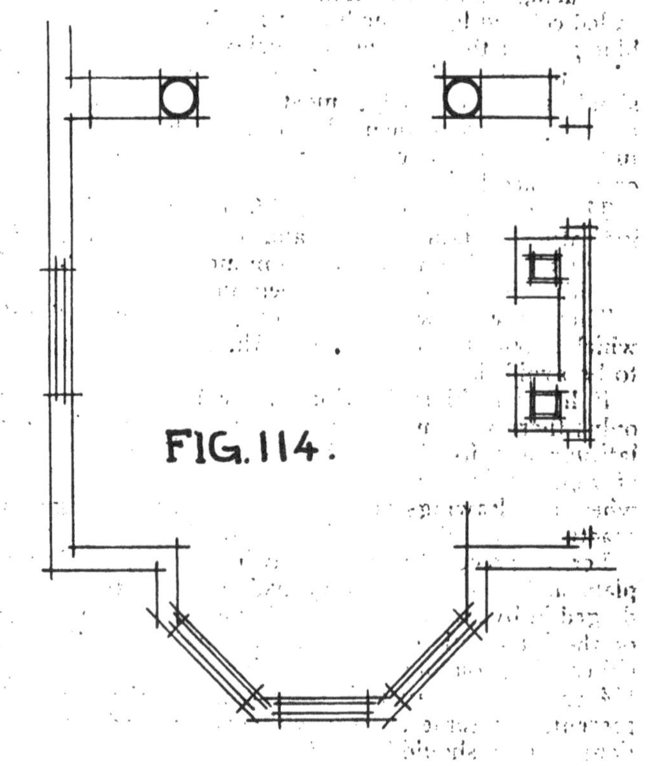

or mutilation of detail—why then should such practice prevail in the making of Plans? Such practice is not only useless but absolutely without justification. Lines so extended are meaningless and to the novice, misleading. They add greatly to the confusion of lines particularly if hatching is the medium of rendering. This is particularly the case when drawings are

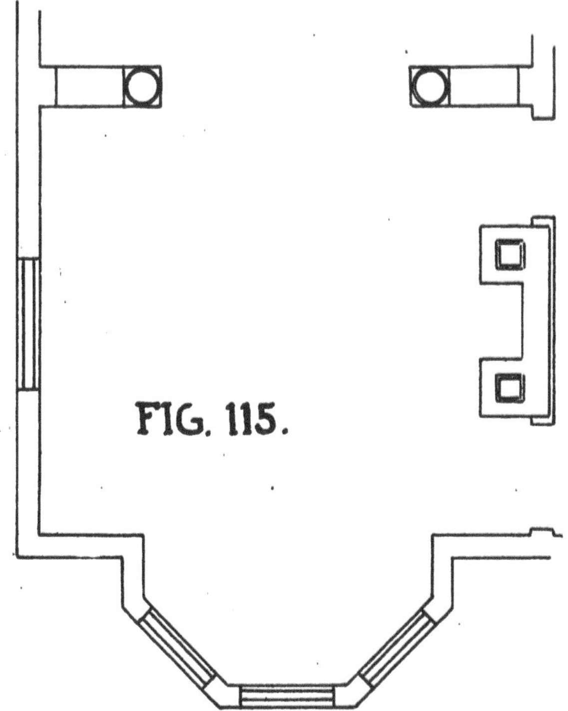
FIG. 115.

made on a small scale. It is a mere fad, apparently a school fad which cannot point to a precedent among the "old-masters" or any standard work on architectural methods.

It is therefore a thing to be avoided.

It is a bad practice to draw small circles around figures on plans promiscuously. It is another useless fad. Circles have their use and meaning; for example: in making an architectural survey, when **heights** are to be indicated on a **plan** the figures representing that height are enclosed in a circle, and because of the particular distinction so given, they are read for what they are worth, without confusion with measurements of flat or horizontal surfaces.

It is bad practice to put any false line on a working drawing, or any drawing made as a guide by which work is to be done. Every line should have a value, and if it possesses none, omit it.

Do not crowd too many drawings or views, on one sheet of paper. Keep each and every detail part separate and distinct from all others. Remember they are to be read by others, perhaps practical men, and should not in any way be confused so as to render that reading difficult or in any way uncertain. This crowding of many things on one sheet is a great mistake, but one made by many compilers of architectural details, which are published in book form for the convenience (?) of the architectural draftsman.

Chart XXVII. Figure 116. Presents a few of the conventions which the beginner should know about. This chart and the one which will follow it, may be used as auxiliary studies for practice by the student. To the teacher, they will probably suggest a type of chart to supplement those of a regular course. A keener understanding and appreciation of these conventions and their intrinsic worth is conveyed to the mind of the student best by the practical application of them.

Example 1: Is a simple geometric figure composed of **right lines.** Such lines, as here made use of are called **contour lines.** That is: They are lines which

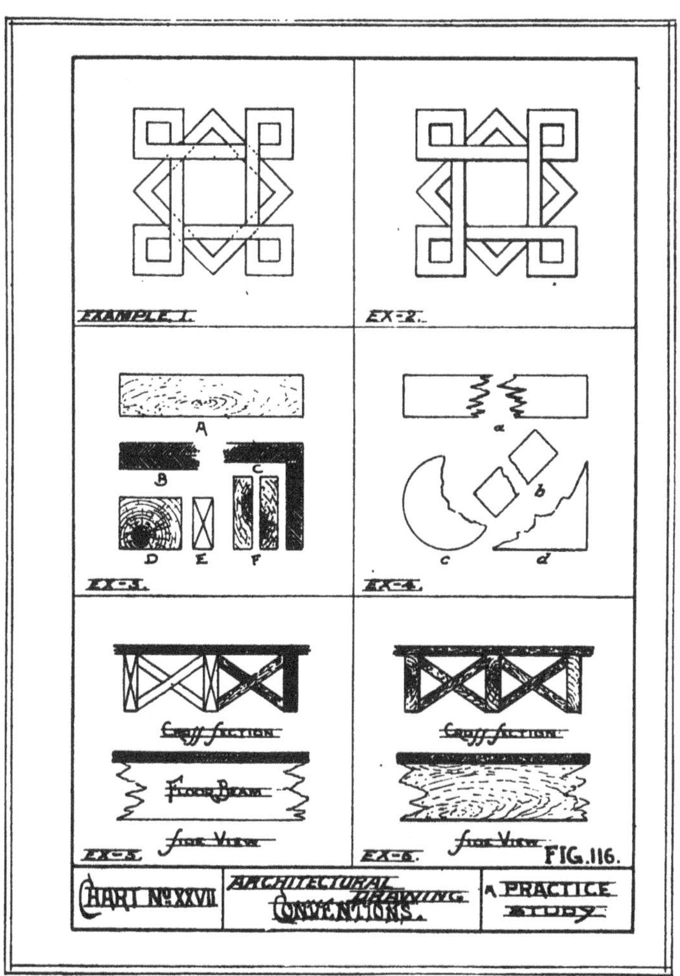
EXAMPLE 1.
EX-2.
A
B
C
D
E
F
EX-3.
a
b
c
d
EX-4.
Cross Section
Floor Beam
Side View
EX-5.
Cross Section
Side View
EX-6.
FIG. 116.
CHART No XXVII
ARCHITECTURAL DRAWING CONVENTIONS.
A PRACTICE STUDY

represent form, either surfaces or solids. There are two systems of contour lines; **Visible lines** and **invisible**, or concealed lines. Visible lines are those which are necessary to represent an object or such part or parts of an object as have nothing intervening between it and the eye of the observer. Invisible lines or concealed lines, are those desirable to show the form of such parts, as, under normal conditions, would be invisible because of intervening substance. Such invisible lines are used as a matter of convenience and to assist in the fuller reading of a drawing. In Example 1—The square figure is so drawn, as to represent that it is separate and apart from the interwoven **"fret-work,"** of the figure composed of smaller squares. And the fact that it is beneath the fret—or rather that it is not a part of it, is indicated by dotted lines; (concealed lines). Concealed lines are not always dotted, very often they are full unbroken lines, but in such case they should be much finer than the visible contour lines. Note the over-lapping and underlaying effect of the bands forming the fret composition, which is accomplished by alternately stopping and extending lines. Example 2—Is the same figure, finished or developed with **shade-lines.** The careful observer will note that the fret is very evidently resting on top of the under-laying square. He will also note, that this effect is made the more apparent from the fact that the shade lines of the top-most figure are much more pronounced than is the case with shade lines of the underlaying figure. Note also the emphasis given the woven parts. This simple example gives a comprehensive understanding of the **value** of **shade-lines.**

Example 3: Show systems for **hatching** parts made of wood. Lumber of all kinds. "A," is a representation of "graining" to indicate a flat view or **surface** of material. "B," shows the method of hatching two or more parts connected, in such manner that it may be clearly understood that while each are separate and apart from the other, nevertheless they are united in construction. "C," a similar example, where the parts stand relatively different to each other. (The principle is the same). "D," shows a sectional view of a stick of **timber**, an end view, as if the stick had been cut with a "cross-cut" saw. The circles represent the **growth-rings** of the tree from which the stick was cut. The radiating lines (which gives the thing the appearance of a spider's web) are "season checks." "E," another way of representing an end wood section. This is the symbol for suggesting end grain, which is most commonly made use of. It is quickly made and equally expressive. "F," another form of representing sticks of timber similar to "D." Example 4: Represents "broken sections," a subterfuge which is very useful, where available space is in sufficient for the drawing of the object in full dimensions. When such breaks are made they should approximate that which would result in a natural way, if the material was actually broken. Some forms of lines used to represent breaks are very easily mistaken by the novice, for contour lines. "a"—Represents a break in coarse-grained wood, also the ordinary varieties of soft wood. Such wood naturally splinters more or less, which fact justifies a very jagged line. "b"—Shows a break in hard-wood or material with more compact and closer grain, or material of a brittle nature. It may represent close-grained wood, brick, terra-cotta, stone, lath and plaster, and substances of like nature. Sheet metal and glass breaks, might be represented somewhat as shown in "c" and "d."

Example 5: Shows the method of applying these symbols in actual practice. Floor-beams, laid with flooring-boards, and braced with "**cross-bridging.**" Two systems are shown for representing the ends of timbers (beams) either of which may be used, but **one style only** should be used on the same drawing. The cross-bridging is shown in surface view; hatched with short, straight lines, in a somewhat parallel direction. This is simply an alternate for the system of graining as shown at "A," Ex. 3. Example 6: Is the same thing more fully developed by hatching. It is further embellished by shade-lining, which clearly indicates that the cross-bridging stands back, or recedes from the end cut of timbers and flooring boards. The side view shows a method, in detail, of indicating individual boards in the flooring (tongued and grooved); each board is shown by lines running in a contrary direction. Example 3: Will make clear the use of all symbols in this connection.

Chart XXVII. Figure 117: Deals with the symbolic Code most commonly used by architects (when used). A—Represents two methods of showing sectional views of stone work (rough stone work), walls, etc. B—Indicates stone of a finer texture, "**cut-stone**" trimmings, etc. C—A variation of the last example consisting of single, full lines, used to represent brick work in section, walls, etc. D—Concrete: A representation of broken stone, by irregular shapes small in size, (crushed stone will assume an endless variety of shapes). The dots between the shapes, are used to represent the sand and cement, filling the **voids** between the cracked stone particles comprising the "**aggregate**" (mass).

E—A **rustic** or **rubble** wall of stone, rough hewn stone or field stone. Such work may be represented either in section or elevation by the same system. Observe that each stone is fully drawn, independent of all others; that is, a line is drawn completely around each stone, not merely finished up to and stopping against another stone. This gives individuality to the stones and at same time a suggestion of mortar joints and bed. F—Shows stone "ashlar" cut, quarried stone, backed with brick, and thus making a compound wall. One of the stones projects into the wall, or brickwork, more than the others which indicates a method of "**bonding**" with "binders." G—Is a simple brick pier of 8" face, or it may be the end view of an 8" wall. The horizontal lines are drawn 2½" apart to indicate the thickness of a common (the average) brick, and the necessary joint of mortar. Two courses to 5". Three =7½", and so on. H—A 12" brick pier or end view of a 12" wall. Bricks are shown alternately as **stretchers** and **headers** 8" and 4" respectively.

I—A section of a stone wall with a "**wash-course**" of cut stone, and a "coping" (capping) of same material. J—Brick wall with stone "**base-course.**" The "**footing**" to the brickwork is "**stepped-out**" for the purpose of increasing the bearing surface of brickwork above. K—A brick pier, 12" face with stepped footing and a concrete base, also cut-stone binder or "**bond-stone.**"

L—An 8" brick pier with rough bond stone, and a double course base of building stone, quarried or field.

M—A sectional view of a well laid or well bonded rubble wall of stone, with concrete base; an application of E.

N—An example to be avoided; It represents an inferior type of stone wall; all the joints in it are bad, and would produce an unsafe wall with total dependence on the footing. Such a wall lacks **bond.** Therefore it should never be drawn like this, unless the draftsman desires to assume responsibility for unsafe construction. The particular stone marked

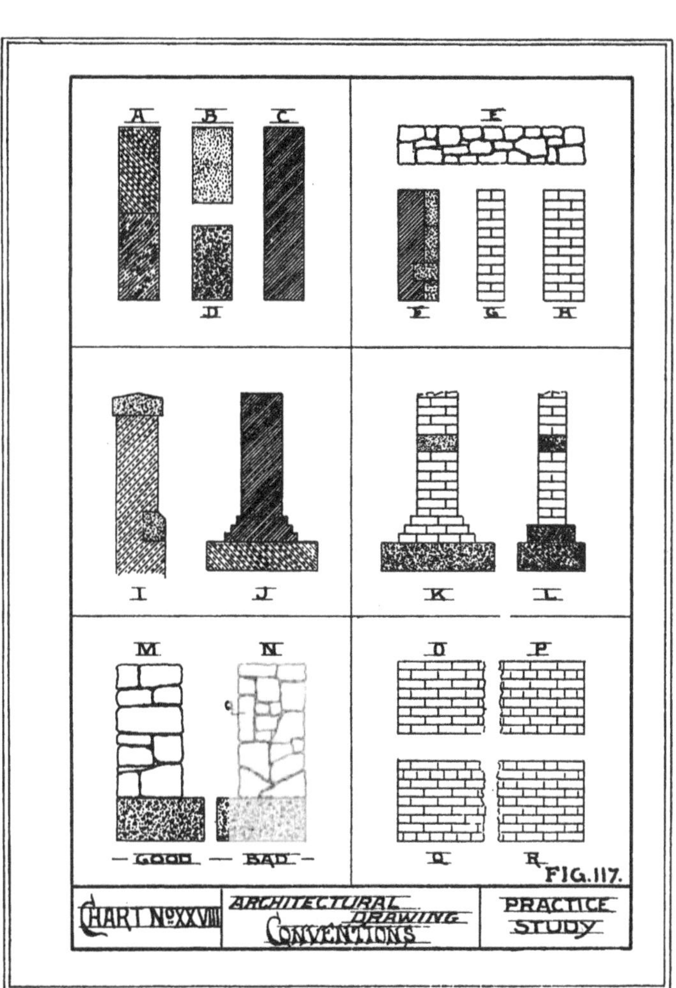
A
B
C
E
D
F
G
H
I
J
K
L
M
N
GOOD
BAD
O
P
Q
R
FIG. 117.
CHART NO. XXVIII
ARCHITECTURAL DRAWING CONVENTIONS
PRACTICE STUDY

"Q" is what is known as a "quaker."* It is a thin stone standing on edge, for the purpose of presenting a commendable **face**, while the **bed** is insufficient to insure bonding. The stones on the top of wall as drawn, give the appearance of a well-built wall, but they are a mere mask.

O, P, Q, and R—Represents face views of different systems of laying or "bonding" brick. O—is what is known as a "running-bond" or "common-bond"; A type much used in America for common work.

P, and Q—Are two systems of what is known as "English-bond." The first consists of alternate courses of stretchers and headers, while the second consists mainly of stretchers with an occasional course of headers.

R—Represents that which is known as Flemish-bond. It differs from the English in that it consists of headers and stretchers, alternating in each course horizontally; and headers and stretchers alternating perpendicularly, i. e., there is at all times a header directly over a stretcher.

There are many systems for bonding brick, but the examples herein given will suffice for the purpose of this book.

*The author does not know the origin of the application.

AFTER WORD.

It has been the purpose of the author to make the context of this book perfectly clear and intelligible to the mind of the average student, and for that reason (or to that end) a **compendium** style has been adopted. However, perfection in this life is a commodity rarely met with, and it is possible, even probable, that the intent may fall short of desired results in some particular instance or in some particular detail.

If so, it will give the author much pleasure to augment this book by correspondence, with such elucidation as may be desired by any reader. Therefore, teachers of drawing or students are hereby privileged to communicate with the author concerning the subjects herein treated, and in acknowledgment, the author will make further effort to remove any veil which may seem to exist.

The author has had no intention of delving into the abiss of technical construction. That has been done in many books which have been published previously, on the subject of "architectural drawing." It has rather been the purpose of the author to **Teach How to Draw**; and such constructive detail as has been shown or referred to, is merely incidental and necessary adjunct to facilitate the teaching.

The **Technique** of **more advanced work** in connection with **Architectural Drawing** will be treated in a book to follow this, in which Practical Constructive Detail will also be more fully considered and explained.

All communications should be addressed to the author, care of The Adams Press, Agents, 62 William Street, New York City (Room 42).